TO WRITE A POEM....

by Len Roberts

TO WRITE A POEM....

by Len Roberts

Copyright © 2004 by Joshua Press

ISBN-0-9725964-0-2

Printed in the United States of America
Published by Joshua Press
Philadelphia, Pennsylvania

ACKNOWLEDGMENTS

Chapters One ("Images"), Five ("How to Begin"), Six ("How to   Continue"), and Seven ("How to End") were published in whole or in part in *TEACHERS & WRITERS* 22, No. 2   (November-December, 1990).

Chapter Thirteen ("First Line/Rhythm Poems") was published, in a slightly revised form, in *SING THE SUN UP: CREATIVE WRITING IDEAS FROM AFRICAN AMERICAN LITERATURE,* Ed. Lorenzo Thomas. New York: Teachers & Writers Collaborative, 1998.

Drawing on cover, "Kite," is by Joshua Roberts.

TABLE OF CONTENTS

FOREWORD

The goal of this book is to help teachers teach their students to write poetry--quickly, simply, effectively, and enjoyably.

Part One discusses four elements that are considered basic to the poem-making process: images, line breaks, comparisons, and word-music. Sample poems at the end of each section provide teachers and students with illustrative models.

Part Two contains practical information on how to help the students begin, continue, and end a poem. Again, sample poems are included to provide models for practice.

Part Three consists of various exercises that will inspire the student to write. These exercises, such as writing a Print Poem, a First Line/Rhythm Poem, or a Place Poem not only provide the beginning writers with a starting point, but, hopefully, they also encourage them to go beyond the exercise and to start writing from their own imaginative core. These exercises are arranged in a suggested sequence only because I have found such an order to be helpful (as comments within the chapters will explain), but they may be used in any order.

These suggestions and exercises are geared for students in grades K-12, but they also have worked successfully with college, and graduate students, as well as with teachers, prisoners, nursing home elderly, and published poets.

BEFORE WRITING

Poetry is Word Play:

The primary goal of teaching children to write poems, and thus of this book, is to show them how working with language can be enjoyable and rewarding. Writing poems should be fun for the beginning writers, an activity which enables them to experiment with language in new ways and consequently to start experiencing their lives in new ways. They should not be trying to write a great poem, nor should they be trying to write a "passable" poem. They should be writing to say what they want to say, and to enjoy saying it. As W.H. Auden once said, a poet is someone who likes to play with words, and this sense of play is what will attract and sustain the beginning writer.

Part of this enjoyment comes from the sharing of their poems, so I mention at the start that, hopefully, some of the writers will read their finished poems at the end of the sessions. If they don't want to, that's fine, too, but I emphasize that poetry is an oral art and that a poem should be heard as well as read. At this point I also suggest that they might want to share their poems as they write them. This sharing is a natural act and usually occurs whether I suggest it or not, but I like the beginning writers to know that they do have the freedom to speak their poems aloud and to share them with their friends even as they are created.

Two Ground Rules: Free Verse and Poetry as Process

Free Verse:

Then I set a few ground rules for the writing session, the first of which is that we try to write without using rhyme. Some of the students may be surprised at first and may resist, but nearly all of them will willingly abandon rhyme within the first five minutes of the session once they have been told it is all right to do so. One major reason for writing without strict meter or rhyme is to avoid rigid structures that inhibit the students' ability to express themselves, often forcing them to write the word "blink" because it rhymes with "sink," rather than finding the word that best expresses their thought and feeling.

Another reason for writing without strict meter or rhyme is that the students tend to write more serious, personal poetry with free verse. Instead of concentrating on the requirements of form, they express themselves more easily and powerfully. Finally, I explain that most contemporary poets do not rhyme their poems, that, in fact, most of the great American poems written in the Twentieth Century do not rhyme. Once the students realize that free verse is an important, accepted form in which to write poems, they take to it naturally and enthusiastically.

(When the students are comfortable with creating in free verse, they may be able to write verse with some success, but, again, I stress that they avoid rhyme for the beginning sessions. There may be some exceptional students who can write rhymed poetry well even though they are beginning writers; those students should be encouraged to continue doing what they do well.)

Poetry as Process:

Students should approach poetry writing, as every other kind of writing, as a process, and therefore I suggest they do not worry about spelling, grammar or sentence structure during the heat of composition. The important thing is to put down whatever comes to them. Later, when they revise, they may look up the spelling of a word or check their comma usage.

There is no great need to belabor these points initially, but it is important to mention them and to continue reinforcing them throughout each work session.

PART ONE: THE BASIC ELEMENTS OF A POEM

CHAPTER ONE: IMAGES

IMAGES

One of the first things I do with beginning writers is to help them to think concretely, in terms of images, which are specific sensory details. Poems use such concrete details to stimulate our senses because we perceive the world through what we see, hear, smell, taste and touch; if writers wish to re-create their experiences, they need to provide the sensory details of that experience. Such re-creation will enable readers to re-live the poem/event as though it were happening right there on the page.

If students don't use images, their poems will consist of general statement after general statement, which will read more like a poorly written essay chopped into short lines than a poem. To help them avoid "general" writing, I show them how to create images.

Image Exercise

One useful image exercise is what I call the Bird or Flower Exercise. Ask the students if the word *bird* is an image. If they answer yes, ask them what bird they see in their minds. They may answer *parrot, sparrow, parakeet, bluebird*, et cetera, but the important thing is that they have moved from the general to the specific in their thinking, a move that will be paralleled in their writing. If the students say the word *bird* is not an image, then ask for an image of a bird, which will lead to the same answers as above. John Blazeck, a third-grade writer, created the following image, which, later, he extends:

Cardinal

Cardinal on my desk

        ****

I usually work with such imaging until the students not only name a specific bird but also begin to
start describing it and its surroundings, which is what I call "extending the image."

Extending the Image: Birds

The next step is to encourage the students to extend the image as much as possible. So, when a student says *cardinal*, ask where the cardinal is: On a white post? A black Mercedes? A snow-covered hedge? And then ask what the cardinal is doing: Is he cracking a seed open in a light rain? Is he flapping his wings in the blue spruce? Is he staring back into the window where the student is staring out? These kinds of questions will cause the beginning writers to think of images in context, and will thus help them to continue writing about the image that they have conjured up. Other questions that may help to extend the bird image might be, "Is the cardinal doing anything unusual? Is it raining or snowing? What else do you hear as you watch the cardinal?" And so on.

Note: I often try to use seasonal descriptions with the image, so, if it is autumn, I'll ask if the bluejay is squawking in the red leaves, or, if it is winter, if the cardinal is flaming on the snow-topped hedge. The students are keenly in tune with seasonal changes and subsequently create some vivid image extensions.

John Blazeck extended his cardinal image to:

Cardinal

Cardinal on my desk
                         flying
                               through the pages
                                           of a book.

Martin Lewis, a fourth-grade student, also extends a cardinal image in his poem:

The Cardinal

The cardinal sounds like my
        Dad when
              he rises
in the morning
        while
             my Mom fries
        eggs for me
             and the sun
makes me feel like I'm sitting
        on a bright red
              fire truck
that's racing to a raging fire.

          ****

Stepanie Laub, a seventh-grade writer, brings the cardinal into her poem after some vivid description:

The Cardinal

Rolling through the field,
white petals caught in my hair,
I topple over the rows
of gleaming white lilies,
pause a moment
to look up in the sky
where a fire-red
cardinal passes by,

cardinal without a care in the world.
It really put things
   into perspective.

   ****

Extending the Image: Flowers

The Flower exercise follows the same procedure as the Bird exercise, beginning with asking if the word *flower* is an image. If the students say yes, ask what flower they see in their minds and they will answer *tulip, rose, dandelion* and so on. Then help them to extend their flower image by asking what color their flower is, where it is, what time of day or night it is, and so on. Again, this kind of questioning prepares the students to get in the habit of extending the image, and thus it helps their poems to develop.

Both Stephanie Laub and Joy Bacher extend their flower images in original, interesting ways:

Streaks of Light

Adjusting my eyes
from a sound sleep,
I see a soft, pale blue carnation
as dew drops fall onto
its dead petals
surrounding
the crystal-clear vase,
the morning sun
gleaming,
leaving streaks of light
on the white, leather armchair.

   --Stephanie Laub, seventh grade

   ****

Milkweed Pods

Milkweed pods grow
along fence posts
all fluffy
and full
like the soft down of feathers,
gentle, misty clouds
that angels might stand graciously upon.

   --Joy Bacher, third grade

9

****

Since images are the basic building blocks of a poem (I often liken the images of a poem to the bricks of a wall), I encourage the students to practice portraying clear images of all types, sometimes reading them ancient Chinese poems, which are highly imagistic, as models. Once the students are convinced that images are fabulous/poetic, they will have taken their first steps toward writing good poems. A few short Image Poems follow:

Smoke

    rising
from a red-bricked
    chimney,
    in little
     white
     puffs.
  Then slowly,
    slowly
disappearing into the
    dark
   evening
    sky.

   --Kristen Wilson, third grade

    ****

Winter

Snowflakes falling
as lightly as feathers.
Everything is white
and quiet.
Then,
suddenly,
a bluejay
sings
one high
sharp
note.

   --Lisa Siftar, fifth grade

    ****

An easy-to-use exercise that will help the students practice their image-making is the "Goodbye_____, Hello_____" poem, which asks the students to substitute seasons (and their respective images) in the blanks, as illustrated in this poem by Matt Drake, a sixth-grade writer:

Goodbye Winter, Hello Spring

Goodbye peanut-butter cookies in the green tin.
Goodbye dirty slush laying on the curbside.
Goodbye Elsey running down the football field.
Goodbye flashing Christmas lights
on the black lamppost.

Hello baseball on Friday nights.
Hello sunshine beaming on my glasses.
Hello hot dogs blackening on the Sunbeam grill.
Hello Easter and your parti-colored eggs.

Two Pitfalls to Avoid in the Image Extension Exercise: Cliches and Nonsensical Extremes

Avoiding Cliches

When asked for a bird image, several students are likely to volunteer *eagle, hawk,* or *dove,* birds which tend to create cliched responses and writing, for the eagle is usually soaring through the sky and the hawk is usually searching for prey; the dove typically coos gently by some flower. (For the Flower exercise, roses tend to create generic responses unless the students are asked what a rose sounds like, a technique discussed in *Chapter Three, Comparisons.*) To avoid these cliched images and thus prevent the resultant cliched writing, ask the students to name birds they see every day, such as pigeons, sparrows, blackbirds, wrens, et cetera.

It always surprises me how readily they name these birds, which, in addition to providing a more original bird-image, also provides the student with contexts for extension. For example, they might see a pigeon by the railroad track on a rainy dawn (because they actually have seen this pigeon there!). Thus they might more easily continue the poem by saying what the train does next, or if the rain turns to hail, and so on. Another valuable aspect of this more realistic, daily image is that it helps the students to "own" the poem; they know this bird, it's theirs, and so they *want* to write about it.

Cliches should also be avoided in image extensions, so that sparrow should not always be in a tree, singing, or on the grass, pecking. I encourage the students to place their birds or flowers in natural yet somehow surprising locations, such as the blackbird strutting beside the yellow maple leaf, or the sparrow on the barn's white gutter. The white rose should not always be in the garden, but should also be lying alone on the Buick's front seat, or in the blue vase glimmering in sunlight. Again, once the students start to claim the birds and flowers as their own, and then put them into their authentic locations, the results will be original, expressive poems.

Note: William Carlos Williams, one of our century's finest imagist poets, had a certain affection for the sparrow in his poems. Two examples are "Sparrows among Dry Leaves" and "The Sparrow". Students are impressed when they hear that a famous poet wrote poems about the common sparrow, and, when time permits, I read the shorter "Sparrows among Dry Leaves" or a section of the longer "The Sparrow" to them.

Sparrows among Dry Leaves

The sparrows by the iron fence post--
hardly seen for the dry leaves
that half cover them--
stirring up the leaves, fight
and chirp stridently, search and
peck the sharp gravel....

****

Here are several lines from Dr. Williams' longer poem, "The Sparrow":

Once
   at El Paso
       toward evening,
I saw--and heard!--
   ten thousand sparrows
      who had come in from
the desert
   to roost. They filled the trees
      of a small park. Men fled
(with ears ringing!)
   from their droppings,
      leaving the premises
to the alligators
   who inhabit
      the fountain....

****

The students enthusiastically relate to the common, everyday quality of Dr. Williams' sparrow poems, and this greatly encourages them to create similar (previously unimportant?) details in their own poems, thus helping them to avoid cliches.

Avoiding Surrealistic Extremes

On the other extreme of cliched response lies the surrealistic response, the student who wants to put his sparrow on a rocket ship and send it to Mars or wants to paint his turkey with seven different color stripes and bury him. Although such surrealistic writing may fare well with accomplished writers, they usually deteriorate, with beginning writers, into fragmented, dissociated images that strive to be jokes rather than authentic expressions. (When this kind of response is given, I gently ask the students to not put their bird or flower on a rocket ship to Mars, but to keep it on the earth, where we can see, hear, smell, taste and touch it better.)

Reality Is Fabulous Poems

Many of these students like to write such fantastic images because they think that's what poetry is; once they understand that, as Thoreau pointed out, reality itself is fabulous, and that they can represent that wonder by merely creating a slightly unexpected image extension, they then accept the idea wholeheartedly, as the two following poems demonstrate.

American Gothic

Standing here
next to my beloved husband
with the sharp whispering pitchfork
in his trembling hand
I feel like telling him
in his open ear
to look up
at the bluebird
sitting in the big oak tree
standing up so brightly
in the purple sun.

   --Heather Glaal, 4th grade

   ****

Sap

As I was standing in my dining room
pouring a cup of tea,
a drop fell to the edge
of the table.
It's like sap,
beautiful,
dripping from a young maple tree,
so thick,
slowly falling,
like an amber bead
hanging from a thin piece of string.

--Monica Sweigard, 4th grade

****

Writers, students or not, sometimes do not know what they want to write about, but if they can start with an image that, through extension, leads to another image, they will eventually discover what it is they want to express. This process of discovery will also free the writers from the frequent problem of not knowing what to write about. They do not have to. All they need to do is to begin with an image, extend it, and then, perhaps, discover what the poem may tell them. Thus, the writing becomes an exciting process of discovery rather than a boring report of known information. This sense of discovery is a great part of the joy of writing.

Revision Examples of Poems Written Before and After the Image (and Line Break) Exercise

Before: *The Garden*

I like it when the wind blows the leaves of the trees back and forth, when the sun is shining bright on the beautiful flowers, seeing the butterflies going past with their bright colors, and the bees going to flower to flower. I like to sit in the grass and listen to the birds while I read a good book. Then before I leave I always pick some flowers for my mom and walk peacefully home.

--Rebecca Crowe, 6th grade

****

After: *Me as a Spider in the Garden*

Walking over the watermelon
I can hear its seeds
growing,
and an ant
crying
under the bright red tomatoes.
I can see the caterpillar
thinking
whether or not she
should be a monarch butterfly,
a black and yellow beauty.
Then I hear music,
the grasshoppers
playing
their violins with their
feet and legs,
all the other bugs
dancing.

Just before I was going
to dance with the other bugs
my mom called me
for dinner
so I had to run
over the raspberries, strawberries,
the plump red tomatoes,
bumpy cucumbers, bright carrots
and finally the big, juicy
watermelon,
where I had started from,
all that running
sure making me hungry.

   --Rebecca Crowe, 6th grade

     ****

The revised poem's specific images allow the writer and reader to participate more fully in the experience being re-created, and I think that's why the verbs in the revised draft become so much more active. Even as they write, the students register this increased excitement and involvement that the particular images give them, an excitement shown by a general liveliness and genuine interest.

Summary

If students start with a unique image from their daily lives that they can relate to, such as a pigeon or violet, they will be able to extend it by describing where it is, what it's doing, et cetera. The more unique and authentic the image and setting, the less cliched the resultant poem, so students should be encouraged to begin with images they know well (sparrow, not eagle), and to make their images as interesting as possible (sparrow beside the blossoming yellow tulip, not on the grass). Given the proper starting image, students will create vivid, interesting Image Poems.

CHAPTER TWO:

LINE BREAKS

LINE BREAKS

After practicing image making, the students are beginning to think more concretely and, while they are still excited, I present another necessary element of a poem: line breaks. First, I go to the board and draw a rectangle with lines to represent a piece of paper. It looks like this:

Then I say, "This is what a paragraph looks like, isn't it. The words begin on the left and go all the way to the right, and then they start on the left again and continue." They agree, one of the students sometimes pointing out that I've forgotten to indent or to leave margins, which I immediately do. I then draw another rectangle, but this time with lines that are short, medium and long, lines which are placed anywhere I want them to be on the page, as shown below. I say, "This is what a poem may look right, right?" When they agree, we can discuss the making of lines in a poem.

Since the first drawing is of a paragraph (prose) and the second is of a poem, I ask the students how the poet knows how many words to put on any given line and how he or she knows where to locate the line. This is a difficult question and it may take the students a while before one answers that the line length and placement are determined by the poet's breath. If the students don't get to this conclusion within a few minutes, I help them by asking them to listen to some words I am about to say and to tell me how many lines of poetry they should be. Deliberately emphasizing the breath pauses, I read certain lines aloud, repeating them as necessary. One example is "The cardinal soars low over the moaning fields." I might read the line as:

The cardinal soars
   low
over the moaning field,...

or I might read it like this:

The cardinal
    soars low
over the moaning

field.

There are, of course, many ways of reading the line; the important aspect is that the students listen to the breath pauses and begin to recognize them. As they say how many lines the words should be, I write them on the board so they can see the poem forming. While doing this, I ask them if the lines should begin flush left, be in the center, or anywhere else along the page. They enjoy doing this and they are, at the same time, beginning to hear the rhythms of words in lines.

A good example of such line breaking for different emphases and effects is seen in William Carlos Williams' poem, "To a Poor Old Woman," which many young writers greatly enjoy:

To a Poor Old Woman

munching a plum on
the street a paper bag
of them in her hand

They taste good to her
They taste good
to her. They taste
good to her

You can see it by
the way she gives herself
to the one half
sucked out in her hand

Comforted
a solace of ripe plums
seeming to fill the air
They taste good to her

****

Dr. Williams' breaking of the lines in stanza two serve to emphasize both the meaning and sound of the end-words, thus showing the reader several perspectives on the same sentence. When I use this poem as a model for students, I point out that the first use of the sentence is presented in one line (l. 4), as is his last use of the sentence (l. 15), and that the two variations (ll. 5, 6, and 7) serve to emphasize, through line breaks, different ideas within the sentence; line 5 emphasizes the *good* taste, and line 6 emphasizes the *taste* itself. This kind of model encourages the students to experiment with their own line breaks and end-words.

MORE ADVANCED WORK WITH LINE BREAKS

Although the breath-rhythm is the basic determinant of the poetic line, and I'm happy if the students master the concept, there are other factors to consider, such as the sound of the last word of the line (end-word) and whether or not the line should be enjambed or end-stopped. These are relatively sophisticated techniques and I do not mention them until the students are happily writing poems and are at a point where they want to learn other methods of line-breaking, perhaps with their second or third writing exercise.

End-Words:

The end-word is the most emphatic word of a line, both musically and logically, for it receives a great deal of attention. The reader sees and hears it more than other words in the line. Because of this emphasis, the writer may want to end a line with a word that echoes a sound at the end of another line or that echoes a word within the line or within surrounding lines.

Note: Although the music of words (repetition of vowels or consonants in proximate lines) will be discussed more fully in *Chapter Four, Word Music*, we need to understand the terms assonance and consonance at this point, so we may see how they play a major role in deciding where to break a line.

Assonance and Assonantal Rhyme:

The repetition of a vowel sound in words that do not repeat the following consonant sound is called assonance; for example, *beep-sweet, flight-high, pay-late,* et cetera. Assonance, when it occurs in end-words, creates what is called assonantal rhyme (which is also called, more generally, slant rhyme, near rhyme, imperfect rhyme, or half rhyme).

Here is an example from Jeff Rinker, a fifth grade writer, which demonstrates assonance in some end-words, thus creating assonantal/slant rhyme:

Walking Along the Beach

Walking along the beach
with cool breezes
from all directions
and waves crashing against my feet
like ice cold water from heaven
with hermit crabs all around me.
Where are they from?
I don't know
and I don't need to know
as they wander off
into a world
of their own.

Jeff emphasizes the long e vowel sound of *beach, breezes, feet* and *me* through his line breaks in the first stanza. The short *o* of *from* and *off* in stanzas two and three then occur, with the long *o* vowel sound taking over, a sound he again emphasizes through line breaks, with *know, know,* and *own.*

Another example of assonantal rhyme occurs in "emerald blues," by a seventh grader, Sheila Janofsky. This poem is more heavily enjambed than "Walking along the Beach," and part of the severe enjambment is due to the writer's placement of the short *i* sound in end words.

emerald blues

looking through
the jeweler's window
I hear echoes off
quarry walls,
granite
glinting facets
as the flutist
sits
on the brink
playing trills,
baroque embellishments.

****

The poem begins with what appear to be o vowel sound echoes in the end words of the first three lines, but which, strictly speaking, do not echo each other. However, the strong short *i* sound of the last seven words makes the poem ring, literally, with echoes, just as the content seems to do. If I were to work with this student again, I might suggest that she try to put a word or two with a short *i* vowel sound at the beginning of the poem, also, to create a stronger musical unity (*looking* is a step in the right direction here).

Assonance often occurs in words other than end-words, creating echoes of sound that are subtle but strong. For a fuller discussion of internal assonance, please see *Chapter Four, Word Music*.

Consonance and Consonantal Rhyme

The repetition of a consonant sound in words which do not repeat the preceding vowel sound is called consonance, and it is another way to create the musical echoes at the ends of lines, thus creating consonantal (or slant) rhyme.

Brandie Hawk, a seventh grade student, creates consonantal rhyme very effectively in her poem, "The River":

The River

Just sitting
  by the clear
  blue river,
I can hear children
    whisper
as the red leaves
    rustle
  in the wind,
I can hear
  giant goldfish
    swimming
in the cool
    water,
  as caterpillars
crawl upon the
  branches
  of the poplars.

****

Technically, this poem has a very interesting and sophisticated structure of sounds, subtle yet persistent and strong. The major sound is the consonantal rhyme of *r* in *clear, river, whisper, hear, water, caterpillars,* and *poplars.* Not only are these nicely interspersed consonantal rhymes, but the poem ends musically on the *r* sound which has carried the poem; a terrific "musical" ending. (For more information about how to end a poem musically, please see *Chapter Seven, How to End.*)

Note: There are also strong vowel echoes in other end words of the poem that create assonantal rhymes. These words are *sitting, river, whisper, wind, goldfish,* and *swimming,* with their short *i* vowel sound. Even though the *i* occurs in the final syllable of only three of these six words, it persists in all six and is heard quite clearly.

To Enjamb or End-Stop a Line

A line may break, then, to stress the music of the end-word, resulting, as it does in most contemporary poetry, in occasional assonantal or consonantal rhymes. There is one more major factor to consider when breaking the line, and that is whether to enjamb or end-stop the line.

Enjambment

Enjambment occurs when the poet 'carries over' a clause or other grammatical unit from the preceding line; it creates a 'run on' line that carries a statement from one line to another without rhetorical pause.   Following is an example of a poem by Jon Eisenberg, a fifth grader, that contains excellent enjambment:

Questions about the Sea

I'm wondering why
is the ocean so
wide, why
the wind tosses
the boat
from side
to side, why
the waves bob up
and why can't we
sail like this forever?

       ****

Jon's poem demonstrates the two major functions of enjambment: to create suspense and flow. The first line, "I'm wondering why," creates a question in the reader's mind about what the speaker is wondering about, and the resultant curiosity pushes the reader onward to the next line, thus creating a flow of words and meaning. The second line, "is the ocean so" creates the same suspense and flow, as do many other lines in the poem. I especially like the penultimate line's enjambment, with the question "and why can't we" being left unanswered till the final line.

The flowing movement created here by enjambment also seems very appropriate to the content of the poem, the recurring "why" that is posited on the recurring waves of the sea, both of which seem to "flow" onward.

"An Angry Morning," by Heather Bush, a fourth-grade writer, also demonstrates enjambment, but this time the overall effect is not so much a smooth flow but a jolting tumbling of words, which again seems to match the poem's content quite well:

An Angry Morning

Anger sounds like
    a ton of bricks
  falling
      out of a
  dump truck
    in Dover
    while
a thousand cars
  honk at each other

                waking me up
                    from a
restless night's
        sleep.

            ****

Here the enjambment emphasizes sound, especially in the first stanza, with the harshness of the *k* creating a good verbal equivalent for the angry emotion: *like, bricks,* and *truck.* The enjambment also creates a ragged effect, with *falling* and *out of a* suspending the reader to the next lines.

Because the *k* sound seems to be so important to this poem's overall music, I would suggest the student revise the second stanza to have the word *honk* at the end of a line, and thus emphasized, and that the word *waking* be revised to *wake* somehow, and that it, too be an end word. Those two small revisions would create a musical unity the poem does not now have, and it would also help the poem to end better.

End-Stop

End-stopped lines occur when both meaning and meter pause at the end of a line. Such pauses mark the completion of a thought and usually, but not always, receive end punctuation. The effect of an end-stopped line is to make the reader pause long enough to comprehend the meaning of the line; it also slows the rhythm of a poem, in contrast to enjambment.

In her appropriately titled poem, "Rising," Barbara Enright, a fifth-grader, creates end-stopped lines which force the reader to take in each line fully before going on to the next, thus emphasizing the images and ideas of the lines:

Rising

Swept up in a dream,
like snowflakes swept on a window,
morning,
awakened,
like a bear after hibernating,
floating on air
as if sinless and soulless,
upward,
as if going through clouds,
rising like an eagle,
soaring in and out,
finally reaching your destiny.

            ****

The end-stops in this poem put much more emphasis on the ideas, such as *swept up in a dream, awakened, as if sinless and soulless, upward,* and *finally reaching your destiny.* Often end-stopped poems will create a more meditative, contemplative mood, as this poem does so effectively.

Becca Tilden, a fourth-grade student, also creates a quiet, meditative mood by end-stopping her lines in her poem, "Sitting in a Meadow":

Sitting in a Meadow

I was there,
me and my buddy sitting quietly
like rocks in my father's meadow,
watching the scared clouds as they changed their shapes
  into fish, boats, and birds.
We sat listening like an alert mother hen sitting on an egg.
We could not hear anything
but the wind swishing through the grass,
like a cat's quiet breath.

     ****

Summary

There are many factors to consider when breaking a line in a poem, including the sounds of the end-words, the desire for a flowing rhythm (enjambed lines) or a halting rhythm (end-stopped lines), but the basic factor is the breath-rhythm the speaker brings to the words of the poem.

In order to hear this rhythm, however, the poet must first hear the sounds of the words that make the rhythm--that is why I continually repeat the words the students say, slowly, clearly, and distinctly, during this exercise. This repetition is a good practice for all of the exercises, but especially so for this one since the students must begin to hear their words as musical units if they are to combine these units into rhythmical phrases. This musical quality of words is discussed in the *Chapter Four, Word Music.*

CHAPTER THREE: COMPARISONS

COMPARISONS

Now the students are using images in rhythmic lines, but much of what they say or write may need to be more imaginative. How can they become more imaginative, to somehow escape the limitations of merely reporting or describing? I use comparison making as a key to their imaginations, a key which will help them to break usual associations and create new, less expected ones. As Aristotle said more than 2300 years ago, a poet's greatest achievement is to be a "master of metaphor," the ability to see similarities between supposedly dissimilar things.

What Does a Rose Sound Like?

To begin, I ask what a rose sounds like, not what a rose looks like or is like, in order to force the beginning writers to make unusual associations and thus free themselves from the strictly logical (and often cliched) response. (For instance, if asked what a rose feels like, many students would respond with "velvet" or some similar, soft material. These usual responses are not possible with what does a rose sound like.)

When asking what a rose sounds like, there are usually literal-minded students who correctly say a rose doesn't sound like anything. In response, I emphasize the use of the imagination and ask the students to imagine what the rose sounds like, always encouraging them to put down the first thing that comes to their minds. If the students are still hesitant, I say my red roses sound like trumpets in the morning when I leave my house, and that they sound like old, tired whispers when I return after a hard day's work. Or, some nights, I'll add, when I go out on the porch to get some fresh air, they sound like the whistling of stars.

Usually students will take to this exercise enthusiastically once they realize it's all right to fabricate, make up, create their responses. In fact, comparison making often evokes a livelier response than the image or line-breaking exercises do, perhaps because the comparisons give them complete freedom for their naturally poetic associations.

The rose comparison may be embellished by asking what color the rose is and by pointing out that a black rose may sound quite different from a yellow rose. The color of the rose often creates the tone or mood of the comparison, with dark colors usually calling forth somber images and brighter colors evoking happier ones. Thus, the teacher may set the tone of the rose-comparison poem merely by selecting the color, as is seen in the following poems:

The Red Rose

The beautiful red rose
sounds like a small baby
  crawling
on the bright green grass.
Now the tiny baby
sounds like a seagull
  crying
on soft, white sand.

When I see this, I feel
like a famous person climbing
a gigantic tree
called poetry,
which is a soft whisper
in the dark night.
Poetry........................
........................Poetry

   --Lisa Strzelecki, sixth grade

    ****

Or this poem, which is more somber, by Clint Rickert, a third-grade writer:

The Black Rose

The black rose
sounds like the death
of an old man and
an old woman and
all of their dogs.

A black rose sounds
like dinosaurs
sinking in molten
lava and tar pits,
to be seen no more.

    ****

Extending the Rose Poem by Adding Comparisons, Using the Five Senses, and Making a Story about the Rose

Once the students are enjoying the rose comparison poem, I ask them to start extending their poems by adding more comparisons, by using the five senses (I see the rose now,...), and/or by making a story about the rose. (For a more detailed discussion of extending a poem, please see *Chapter Six, How to Continue*.)

Rose Poem Extended by Comparisons

In the following poem, Jacob Rigel, a third-grade writer, extends his rose comparison with two additional comparisons, all three of them being distinctly different.

A Yellow Rose

A yellow rose sounds like a plaid
shirt that has been mended. The good
old woman's hands mending that nice, blue
 and black shirt. A yellow rose sounds
  like two boys playing hopscotch
   on the sidewalk, along Route
         663
      when a Lamborghini
        zooms by.
          A
        yellow
         rose
          is
          a
         per-
         son
        com-
         ing
        home.

            ****

Many of the Rose Poems extended by comparisons can continue even longer than Jacob's, as
"My Periwinkle Rose," by Erin Dolan, a fourth-grader, shows:

My Periwinkle Rose

My periwinkle rose sounds
like: my grandfather's pipe
  and has
the sweet scent of his tobacco.
The vibrance of its opening
  is deafening
like a match loudly glimmering
in the eerie glow
of a child's moon
as a cardinal signals
its bugle-like call,
an awakening.
Like: fresh dew
of a morning's
crispness.
Like: a floral dress
on a woman thinking about her life,
when she was a child
dancing in a square,

where she carried a basket,
her own,
filled
with the eggs
of her orange chicken.
Now, like: a trickling
of a fountain
seeming to answer
the cardinal's call,
the purple waters
flowing off the sides
and the scents
of the mint-fresh water,
all
entrancing me
and I react to the agony
of the dying flower,
the one,
musical
and peacefully
dying periwinkle rose.

****

Rose Poem Extended by Using the Five Senses

Here Lisa Strzelecki, a sixth-grade student, extends her poem by using the senses of listening, touching, smelling, eating and seeing.

The Rose Poem

A rose sounds like a delicate princess
    sighing at the world.
Now the princess hears the gentle rose
    whispering its most intimate
    secrets.
When the princess touches the crumbling
    rose, she falls into its dreamland.
The princess in all her royal life has
    never smelled such a beautiful smell
    as the spring-blooming rose.
At the elegant table the princess never
    ate anything as delicious as a winter
    rose.
Oh, but when she sees it!
When she sees the rose

she dances with joy,
with such enthusiasm
only you would know
who nurtured the rose,
cared for it in the cold,
shared its secrets.
The princess and the rose.

****

Rose Poem Extended by Using Transitional Words or Phrases Such as *Now, Suddenly, While*, and others. (Please see *Chapter Six, How to Continue*, for a more detailed discussion of this technique.)

Emily Ficnel, a fourth-grade student, uses the words "while" and "now" to continue her poem:

Imagination

The white rose sounds like
  the wind over a fallen sky
while the black crow watches over
  the now blackened sky of charcoal.
Now comes the parrot of all
  the colorful colors of the rainbow
which brighten the charcoal sky
  in a trance of brilliance.
Screech went the chalk on the
  blackboard as the beautiful
young girl continues to think
  of a poem with the white rose,
black crow, and the colorful parrot
  in her artist-like mind.

****

Rose Poem Extended by Creating a Story

Renee DeHart, a fourth-grade student, extends her poem by making a story that began with a comparison.

The Yellow Rose

A yellow rose sounds like
my sister rolling
in the green grass
of the golden field,

in back of my
little log cabin.

Surrounded by Queen Anne's Lace
    she jumps
and does a belly flop
    over them.

She laughs and rolls
near a rosebush
with long, green, sharp
    thorns
on the green stem
as I watch and listen.

       ****

Other Comparative Terms

When the class begins to tire of the rose-comparison exercise, I turn to other terms of comparisons, some of which are often seasonal, such as *snow,* or *red leaf.* These are usually very successful because the students are so in tune with nature and their environment. Sometimes, to prepare for these poems, I will bring the students outside into the snow, or into a pile of leaves (weather and situation permitting), so they can fine tune their senses and start to see, hear, touch, taste and smell even more sharply. Again, I use "What does the red leaf sound like," or "What does the snow sound like," encouraging the unusual associations. A few seasonal comparison poems follow:

Red Leaves

Red leaves
    fall
  in autumn,
sound like an ant's
  crying
    as he drops
  from the fragile
petal of a violet,
  silence
in which I hear
    my father
    sleeping
  as the coffee
  drips
  from the silver pot.

--Julie Kaufman, sixth grade

****

Red Leaf

A red leaf sounds
like a red ant
   crawling over
an ant lion's tomb,
a chocolate cupcake,
past the NEW YORK TIMES
   headline,
up the white rain gutter,
singing "Chim Chimerie"
   until the sun sets.

--Class collaborative poem, sixth grade

****

Snow also works well, as this short, imagistic poem by Tricia Buckman, a fifth-grader, demonstrates:

Snow

Snow sounds like
A white horse in a field of daisies,
an old man's white beard,
a cloud in the sky,
a white sheet under a Christmas tree
in a room with no furniture,
just blank walls.

****

Other comparative terms I've found effective are jewels, such as diamonds and rubies, probably because of their crystal clarity and sparkling redness. I like to bring in (artificial!) gems for this exercise, so the students can pass them around and observe them carefully, with my encouragement to place their ears to the gems to "listen," or to hold the gems to the sunlight, and so on. In the following examples, the students' poems exhibit definite color associations with the gems, which makes the poems themselves "sparkle."

Diamond

A diamond sounds like

a quartet of trumpets
echoing in an empty church,
the sound bouncing ever so quietly
as the last note diminishes
into the plush, purple carpet.
Bold brass trumpets highlight
  the balcony
as the trumpeters slowly
bring the sanctuary
alive with colors
or orange, red and yellow.

   --Jennifer Ray, seventh grade

       ****

Another diamond comparison poem that works well is "A Diamond," by Anastasia Dietze, a fifth-grade writer:

A Diamond

A diamond sounds like
my grandmother reading Shakespeare
in a small library
with blue forget-me-nots around her,
while a charming young lady
feeds lilacs to doves.

       ****

Kim Habruner, a fifth-grade writer, creates a strong comparison with a ruby in "Red Hot":

Red Hot

A ruby sounds like
a red hot cherry
  burning
in a wine glass
at Christmas.

       ****

After using such specific comparative terms as *leaf, snow, diamond* or *ruby,* I use more abstract terms, such as *time, anger*, or *happiness.*

Anger

Anger sounds like
   a person with a jackhammer
working on the road
while dozens of cars
   honk their horns at him
         until
the screeching of brakes
and a crash is heard.

   --Chris Axarlis, fifth grade

      ****

Time

Time is like
a flow of geese
flying across the blue sky
in the noon of the day
with the wind blowing
across the whole earth.

   --Donna Bellesfield, fourth grade

      ****

Sometimes the students will create their own term of comparison, as Tom Anfuso, a fifth-grade writer, does in his poem, "Fireworks":

Fireworks

Fireworks are like tiny rainbows of fire
bursting and flaring
they can make
a simple boom
or a complex flower
in the night.

      ****

Once students are comfortable with the comparison making, they will experiment with their own methods, creating authentic poems such as this one by Jeanine Machain, a fifth-grade student.

Diamonds and Rubies

Look at the diamonds

and rubies,
like fire and ice.
I picked them up and turned
   them around.
In the diamond I saw a white dove
   flying
through the big, blue sky.
I looked at the ruby
and saw a beautiful cardinal
pecking on a sunflower seed.

****

Summary

There are many comparative terms that may be used for this exercise. I have found working with seasons (*red leaf, snow*), colors, emotions, and jewels to be very effective, but the comparative term used should be custom-created for the particular class in its particular situation and season. Given a term they can connect with, students will truly flex their imaginations.

CHAPTER FOUR: WORD-MUSIC

WORD MUSIC

Words have certain sounds which, when combined properly, can create their own kind of music. Most good writing will contain this musical quality, from the King James Version of the Bible to Herman Melville's *Moby Dick* to the well-written travel essay in *National Geographic*. This musical quality is essential to a poem, for poetry is above all else an oral art, the creation of words to be said or sung aloud with a particular rhythm and sound.

Since the beginning writers will be creating free verse poems, they cannot rely upon full end-rhymes to create the echoing sounds of words so necessary to poetry. They may use slant rhymes, however, relying on assonance and consonance in the end words, as many contemporary poets do, to achieve some of this music. (Please see *Chapter Two, Line Breaks*, for a fuller discussion of such slant rhyming.)

The beginning writers may use assonance, consonance and alliteration within the lines to create their word music, even, at times, creating internal echoes with end words (internal slant rhyme). Before presenting these three basic music devices to the writers, though, I talk a few minutes about the importance of speaking words loudly and distinctly, an ability any poet must have in order to not only read but also to create a poem.

Word-Speaking: Moon and Rock

First I ask them, as a group, to say the word *moon* clearly and loudly. The result, depending on the grade level, ranges from 25 exuberant second-grade voices ringing clearly to 25 mumbled seventh-grade voices trailing off into the classroom air. If the result is strong, I go on. If not, I ask the writers to say the word again, and again, pronouncing the word myself so they will hear its full texture, sometimes exaggerating the *ooooo* sound, drawing it out, sometimes exaggeratedly rounding my lips in a circle to show how the *m* is pronounced, and so on. Although there may be some initial hesitation with this exercise, most students soon wax enthusiastic and it's all I can do to quiet them. This is a good beginning.

Then I ask them to speak the word *rock* aloud, again distinctly and loudly, again modeling the pronunciation, emphasizing the rolling quality of the *r*, the very hard sound of the *ck*.

Once the students have spoken these two very different sounding words clearly and loudly, I ask them what they felt when they said *moon,* if they had any physical reaction to the word as they said and heard it. With luck, one of them will say the word had a rising quality to it, that it was light and floating. (If they don't say this, I do!) Then I ask the same question about the word *rock*, emphasizing its heaviness, its downward movement, its solidness. Then we talk a bit about how the sound of the word moon seems to fit the object itself, round and floating in the air, and how the same seems to apply to the word rock, being so solid and anchored to the earth.

What's most important here, though, is always the fact that they begin to speak and hear words distinctly, that they do not race over the words, thus turning them into indistinct verbal blobs. For only if the beginning writer speaks and hears the individual words will he or she be able to put those words into lines that have word-music, and only then will the writer be able to create a poem. This idea of the word as the basic building block of a poem is essential and I emphasize its importance throughout all sessions: by reading the students' words aloud clearly (modeling), by asking the students to read their words to me quietly (conferencing) or loudly (public reading), always praising the sounds of the words as they chant their way across the page.

Note: If the students are older, and if we have time, I tell them an anecdote about attending a conference where Galway Kinnell, one of our best, Pulitzer-Prize winning poets, was conducting a poetry workshop for graduate students. During the workshop, a student read a poem which was not very imaginative or original, a fact which Kinnell, after the reading, pointed out candidly. However, Kinnell went on to say that he thought the writer might indeed become a poet, because he formed his words so carefully in his mouth, tasting them, Kinnell said, like plump, delicious berries even as they were said. It is this physicality of the word that I try to get the students to speak and hear, a physicality which we seem to be losing every day, perhaps because of television, radio, speed and silent reading, and other developments which lessen the value of the spoken, individual word.

Assonance, Consonance, and Alliteration

Then, using their previous drafts, we discuss the three basic "music-making" devices of words: assonance, consonance, and alliteration.

Assonance

As mentioned in *Chapter Two, Line Breaks*, assonance is the repetition of a vowel sound in words where the following consonant sounds do not repeat; for example, *ride-night, glow-rode, raid-place,* et cetera. When these repetitions occur in end-words, they create assonantal (slant) rhymes, also as mentioned in *Chapter Two*. Assonance also occurs within the lines, however, and it can create a very subtle sense of musical echoing in a poem. Alison Silhanek, a fifth grader, demonstrates good internal assonance in the following poem:

The Violin

A bea*u*tiful instr*u*ment
ringing
like *a* ch*u*rch bell,

its m*u*sic
clear and joyous
like *a* f*u*ll m*oo*n
j*u*mping out of the *u*niverse.

Its strings m*a*de of c*a*t-g*u*t
vibr*a*ting
like *a* gl*a*ss
sh*a*tters
on *a* stone floor.

The long *u* vowel sounds in *beautiful, instrument, music, full, moon,* and *universe* dominate the first two stanzas, with the short *u* vowel sound of *church, jumping,* and *gut* contributing a minor echo. The long and short *a* vowel sounds in *made, vibrating, cat, a, glass, shatters,* and *a* take over in the last stanza, thus creating a strong assonance throughout. (Note: I might suggest to this writer that she attempt, in revision, to create some long *u* vowel sounds in the last stanza, which would give the poem more musical unity.)

Consonance

The repetition of a consonant sound in words which do not repeat the preceding vowel sound is called consonance; for example, *flip-cap, black-knock, trees-miss,* et cetera. It is another way to create the musical echoes both within lines and at the ends of lines. As mentioned in *Chapter Two, Line Breaks*, when these echoes occur at the ends of lines they create consonantal (slant) rhyme. Consonance, like assonance, creates a very strong yet subtle music within the lines, as is illustrated in "Quiet," by a fifth-grade writer, Rosemary Buckendorff:

Quiet

*Si*lence *s*ound*s p*ur*p*le
A*t* La*k*e Wa*ll*en*p*au*p*a*k*.

We *s*tar*e a*t the *s*ilen*t* horizon
A*s* cool ai*r r*ise*s f*rom the wa*t*er,
Enveloping u*s* and the *s*un*s*e*t*
in lilac vapo*rs*.

Our *s*ound*s* lo*st*
In the va*st*, pine-*s*cen*t*ed ai*r*,
We feel the ro*s*y mauve
In ou*r s*oul*s*.

As indicated by the italics, this poem has a strong *s* consonance throughout, and, in the first two lines, a strong *p* and *k* consonance (*purple, Lake Wallenpaupak*). I especially like that the poem ends with a powerful echo of the *s* sounds in the word *souls*, which gives the poem a musical finality.

There are other good consonant sounds in the poem, too, such as the *l* of the first stanza (*silence, purple,* and *Lake Wallenpaupak*), and the *t* and *r* echoes in stanzas two and three (*t* sounds: *stare, at, silent, water, sunset, lost, scented; r* sounds: *stare, horizon, air, rises, water, vapors, air, our.*)

Alliteration

The third and final device that creates sound echoes in words is alliteration, which, technically, is the repetition of sounds, be they vowels, consonants, or syllables. (Assonance and consonance, then, are forms of alliteration.) The most common type of alliteration, however, occurs when the initial consonants of words are repeated within a line or line group, as in *the barber burst the pink balloon.*

Because this type of alliteration is a more obvious music-making device, most contemporary poets do not use it as much as assonance or consonance, but some do use it, and quite effectively. I find alliteration to be a good word-play exercise for beginning writers, for many of them will try to out-do each other with their bombastic buffooneries or their long-lost leaders leaning lowly on ledges. This creates a genuine sense of word-play in the students, which, as W. H. Auden often said, is a valuable and necessary ingredient for a poet. This sense of play is seen in "Diamond," by Howard Naulty, an eighth-grader:

Diamond

          a diamond
*s*ound*s* like a *s*himmering *s*cream
of a lady being *p*u*s*hed into a *p*it
          a*s s*nake*s* at the bottom
hi*ss*ed and *s*hifted their *s*lender
          *s*lithering bodie*s*

          ****

The dominant alliteration here occurs in the *s* consonant of *sounds, shimmering, scream, snakes, shifted, slender, and slithering,* and it works quite well with the snake topic, creating onomatopoeia that makes the reader "hear" the snake as it slithers. There is also a minor alliteration in line three, with the *p* consonants beginning *pushed* and *pit.* As mentioned above, most contemporary poets won't use this form of alliteration often, but it is a wonderful way to get students to begin playing with the sounds of words, as may be seen in the following poem by Diana Silva, a second-grade student:

Hiding

Hiding in my garden
    I can hear
       Time
like a *p*urple *p*assion *f*ruit
    *f*alling *f*rom
a *p*urple *p*assion *f*ruit tree
    in *P*ortugal.

          ****

43

The delightful play on the *p* consonant rings throughout the poem, and the *f* alliteration of line 5 echoes the consonance of *passion fruit*, and gives the poem additional musical echoes.

Revision Example

Here are the first draft and revised draft of "The Tilting December Moon," by Kris Newhard, an eighth-grade writer. Revisions were made primarily to enhance the line breaks and word music of the poem.

Draft

The Tilting December Moon

To Han Shan:

The lush greens swarm
At your feet,
Harsh cold rips your numbness
Overflowing your body
With thought.
Pink blossoms of your tree
Drift alone,
Your fire sparks
In your cold hearth and
The smell of wine
Cascades out with every breath,
The whiskey scorches at your
Throat. Sunken eyes, carefully
Guarded by the tilting December moon.
The river's mist wafts
Over to you until
Your spark has been conquered.

Revised Draft

The Tilting December Moon

To Han Shan:

The lush greens
Swarm at your feet,
Harsh cold rips
Your numbness,
Overflows your body
With thought.

Pink blossoms of your tree
Drift alone,
Your fire sparks
In your cold hearth,
The smell of wine
Cascading out with every breath,
The whiskey scorching at your throat.
Sunken eyes, carefully guarded
By the tilting December moon.
The river's mist wafts
Over you
till your spark goes out.

****

Explanations of Revisions

Line one is broken at *greens* rather than *swarm* in order to get the assonantal rhyme with *feet* of line two and, later, with *tree* of line seven. Line three is broken at *rips* in order to create a consonantal rhyme with *numbness* (now of line four). One of the strongest consonantal rhymes in the first sentence of the poem occurs naturally in the first draft, with *feet* of line two slant rhyming with *thought* of line six.

Line nine has the end-word, *and*, removed so the consonantal rhyme of *r* in *sparks* and *hearth* might be better heard, as well as emphasizing the consonantal rhyme of *th* in *hearth* and *breath* of line eleven. Line twelve has the word *throat* brought up from the following line, so that it will create a strong consonantal rhyme with the greatly revised last line, *Your spark goes out,* with *throat* and *out* echoing strongly to conclude the poem.

Line thirteen brings the word *guarded* up from the following line in order to emphasize the consonantal rhyme of the *r* heard earlier in *sparks* and *hearth*, thus unifying the poem musically. The last revision is in line sixteen, where u*ntil* is changed to *till* and carried down to the next line, in order to emphasize the *u* vowel sound of *you* with *moon* two lines above.

The revised draft has greatly improved line breaks and word music, thus demonstrating how craft can be used to "re-create" words and their various combinations. It's important to remember, though, that this poem could have many other possible line breaks for different emphases and different kinds of music, depending upon the writer's intentions. The important aspect to keep in mind here is that the writer has some notion of craft and is employing it to shape the poem's words in an artful way.

Summary

The sound value of the distinctly spoken word is the very basis of a line of poetry and thus of a poem. Once the students start to speak and hear words, they will be able to combine them into sound-echoing lines which, with luck and work, will form poems. Once they have a draft before them, the devices of assonance, consonance and alliteration will help them to revise for more musical effects, such as substituting a word for its sound value rather than just its denotation. The more the student works with these devices, the more they will show up in their first drafts, for we human beings love language and will try to make it flow whenever possible.

PART TWO: THE PROCESS OF WRITING A POEM

CHAPTER FIVE: HOW TO BEGIN

TO BEGIN

Once the students are enjoying images, line breaks, comparisons, and word music, I ask them to write an "ing" (or participle) poem, using some of the images and comparisons they had written during the class exercises.

Because this is their first full-scale attempt at writing a poem, I try to make it as easy as possible for them by suggesting they write about a special place. (For a more detailed discussion of a Place Poem, please see Chapter Nine, Place Poem.) A teacher could begin with any of the exercises in this book, but the exercise, since it is the first, should be simple and direct.

Select a Special Place

The selected place should be unique and special, and I ask for examples which I then write on the board, encouraging them to "borrow" any place that might inspire their writing. Some of these places might be a rowboat on a lake at dawn, a dusty summer alley, or a carnival on a spring evening, and so on. I encourage them to select places that have strong images, so it will be easier to write the poem once they put themselves "there." If a student chooses a place with few unique or interesting images, such as a bare backyard, such selection will make the poem more difficult to write.

When they name their places, I ask them questions meant to help them extend their core image, such as What time of day/year is it? What do you see, hear, touch, smell, taste there? What do you feel/think in this special place? What colors do you relate to your place? Et cetera.

I also emphasize that it is fine to imagine things at their special place, too, such as a worm eating its way through an apple while they sit in a storming tree house, or the yellow leaves dropping in November like paratroopers, and so on. These imaginings, when combined with the literal descriptions, will create interesting juxtapositions and unexpected associations, good ingredients for a poem.

When the students have plenty of special places on the board and are excitedly mentioning aspects of these places, I read a few Place Poems written by other students their approximate ages, pronouncing the words and rhythms distinctly, modeling the care and attention I would like them to give to their own words. "Skating," a poem by Renee DeHart, a fourth-grade student, is a good one to read at this point:

Skating

  Skating on the pond
     I hear
the light clouds of the night
    moving slowly
as I glide over the blue ice.

  When I look over
to the green pine forest

I see a lily
  blooming like a diamond
sparkling in a deep turquoise sea.

  When I taste the yellow moon
  glistening on my face,
    I reach out
and touch the gleaming star
    that beams down
from the top of a gigantic tree.

  Then I skate
over to the edge
    and make
    a figure eight
  as large and round
  as the entire pond.

     ****

Or, if the students are older, the following poem by Gretchen Alm, a ninth-grade student, works well as an introduction:

Stonehenge

I.

Kneeling in Britain's
stonehouse of the Lord
I hear saints spit
blasphemous epithets
while their graven faces
betray nothing
and silence my eyes.

Dusty light
fills me
with chants.

II.

Holding back a yawn
in the drowsy Downs,
I half-listen for the battle cry
from an Anglo-Saxon warlord.

Sleep cajoles me--
I would sleep forever
but for the color green,
green that throws me back
against a throng of grasses,
push, PUSH me away from this place.

****

Other Pre-Writing Tips

I suggest that they also use the "ing" verb to begin (which will put them directly in the experience), put no more than six words on a line (at least at the beginning of their writing), use specific sensory images as well as imaginings, and, last, that they fill at least one side of a page with writing in the next fifteen minutes. They usually look at me in disbelief when I say this, but by the end of those fifteen minutes most of the students have written the full page. I also remind them at this point not to worry about spelling or punctuation, for those are things they can correct, if necessary, in revision.

Then We Write

While they write, it is essential that the teacher walks around to help those who are stuck, to give encouragement and praise their good efforts. This is so important that, once they've been writing for several minutes, I will ask if anyone is stuck, so I might help that writer overcome whatever is blocking his or her writing. Of course, some of the students will be too embarrassed to raise their hands, so I make sure I check their poems individually as they're being written.

When I come across a particularly good line or image, I will ask the student if I may read it aloud to the class. If the student assents, I read it aloud, again modeling the way the words should be phrased, and praising it. This usually inspires the writers, too, and I encourage them to "borrow" anything they hear that might propel their writing. (These borrowings may be deleted, if desired, during revision.)

I discourage students from leaving their seats or sitting with their hands raised, for such actions only stop them from writing. I assure them I will get to each one of them, and that they should continue to write until I get there. If they have finished one poem, then they should write another. Many of these second and third poems turn out to be the best ones.

It is very important that the teacher get to each student and comments upon that student's efforts while he or she is writing. I have often stopped at a student's desk to find only a few words written, but with a couple of questions and some encouragement, that student will usually continue and finish a poem. For this reason, it is ideal to have no more than twenty students in a writing class, although I know this is usually impossible. Another alternative would be to have another teacher or a parent helping to read the students' writings during the session to ensure immediate feedback.

At the end of the session, the students may hand the poems in, or, if they are not satisfied with their work, they may take them home and revise them. This aspect of revision is very important also, and the beginning writers should not be misled to believe their first efforts are their best efforts. It has been my experience that many of the students want to revise their poems, especially if there is a possibility of a public reading or publication.

The following two "beginning" poems by students demonstrate the participial beginning, use of images from a specific place, and references to the senses.

Quiet Night

Lying in the yard
amongst the wet grasses
I look at the stars.
The air is cold.
The stars shine bright
like little light bulbs at Christmas.
Red, yellow and blue dots
on dark black paper.
I hear the stars whisper
in my ear.
I look to the north
and see the Aurora Borealis,
a veil of green.

--Keith Ohrberg, sixth grade

****

Standing by the Red River

Standing by the river
I can hear
the reddish water rapidly moving
and feel the dead leaves
brushing against my legs
while others amble along the banks
waiting for the bright, hot sun
to go down.
Now all I hear
is the leaves whistling,
and the red river skimming over rocks.
And when I look up
at the pink and blue sky,
I see it's looking down on me.

--Nicole Metzger, fifth grade

CHAPTER SIX: HOW TO CONTINUE

HOW TO CONTINUE

What does a teacher do when the student is stuck, cannot get another word down on paper? This is a very frustrating time for the writer, since the poem began with a promise that seems to be fizzling out. One way to help the student continue writing is image-extension, which is discussed in Chapter One, Images. There are also several other ways: continuation words and phrases, use of the five senses, and repetition of key words and phrases.

Continuation Words and Phrases

One technique that enables the writer to continue writing is the use of continuation words such as *now, suddenly, soon, while,* or other transitional words of time, as is seen in "Dad," by a fifth-grade writer, Todd Eubanks:

Dad

Lying down,
looking up at the stars,
like a fish
looking at his bait,
suddenly
I feel my father's arm
wrap around me.
Hum of the cricket
seems to go down.
The fire dims,
the red sun
sets over the horizon.

****

When using these words, I suggest that the image that comes after the transitional word does not have to logically follow the previous image; in other words, if the first image is about trains, the second image doesn't have to be--it can be about sunflowers, mothers, a trip to the Caribbean, whatever the imagination gives. Nick Wagner, a sixth-grade student, makes such an associative leap in his poem, "The Cornfield":

The Cornfield

In spring as I lay in old Jose's cornfield
watching the warm air fly through the dead brown stalks,
I see crows scattering along in the moist brown topsoil
    searching for worms
while my father, miles away, starts to snore on the couch,
just after coming home from a long day
    at the factory.

****

I especially like the associative leap in Nick's poem between the cornfield and his home because it shows how well he knows his father's routine life, the major point of the poem.

Transitional words and phrases of place, such as here, inside, outside, out in the wheat field, past the oak tree, et cetera, also work well, not only to enable the student to continue writing but also to give the poem a different perspective. For instance, Tori August, a seventh-grader, uses "while on Broad Street" and "Down the street" to keep writing:

Walking Down Ralston Road

I hear robins chirping
way up high in the budding maple
and buzzing bees flying around
the melting ice cream cone
while on Broad Street
the screeching of the red Porsche
makes heads turn toward the teenagers
singing "Motownphilly" by Boyz II Men
as they cruise down the street
where old ladies work neatly in their gardens,
beads of sweat lining their foreheads,
tapping their feet and humming along to the tune
as they bend over in
their red tulip beds.

****

If the writer wishes to change the pace of the poem, words such as *slowly, quickly*, or *surprisingly* work well, as is seen in this poem by Matt Drake, a sixth-grader:

Blue Spring

Walking down Brookline Boulevard
I can hear blue spring
like the crack of the bat
at Three Rivers Stadium.

Slowly
weeps come from
Debor's Funeral Home
while the church bells ring
and old men rest on the benches
near the World War II cannon,

listening to old Bernie
practicing his saxophone
as his beagle barks the melody,
while I walk down Brookline Boulevard.

There are many such words that might be used, and I have found it helpful to put some of them on the board while the students are writing, and I encourage them, if they are stuck, to use one of the words. (Again, I find transitional words of time and place to be the most effective.) If such words detract from the poem, the students may remove them later, when they revise.

Note: Various continuation transitional phrases or sentences may be created for different exercises. For example, in the QUIET poem chapter of this book, one sentence that will help the stuck student to continue writing a Quiet poem is "Now, when I listen very carefully," for the writer will then be able to hear things previously unheard and to write them down. I refer to such continuation phrases and sentences in appropriate exercise chapters.

Continuing through the Five Senses

Another way to help students continue their writing is by asking them to refer to the five senses of seeing, hearing, touching, tasting and smelling. I write the five senses, as well as the words think, feel, and imagine on the board before writing begins, explaining to the students that they may use one or more of the words to continue writing if they get stuck.

Sometimes this approach produces merely a list of sensory comparisons, but more often than not it helps students to add good material to their poems that they otherwise would not have written. And, of course, the reference to the senses themselves may be removed in revision, if the writer so desires. This inclusiveness in a first draft, however, is always something to work for; the writers should write anything and everything that comes to mind, knowing they can remove whatever material they want to in the revision process. They should not censor any word or line that may come, for that might turn out to be the best writing of the entire poem.

Ed Transue, a seventh-grade writer, uses the senses to continue his poem, "The Beach":

The Beach

Walking down the beach
I saw the dead Great White Shark
half buried in the sand.
I walked up to him
and put my ear to his cold, wet
skin,
hearing the endless sound
of silence.
No sound, no movement,
not even the sound
of waves pounding and slapping,

just nothingness.
His mouth partially closed
while his large teeth smiled at me,
looking at me with green eyes
where I could see the still pools
of his pupils, and when I woke
I could still see that same shark
lying there in the silence.

****

I remember stopping at Ed's desk when he was composing this poem, and he was stuck after writing the third line, "half buried in the sand." I asked him to somehow use the sense of touch next, ensuring him that it would help him to continue, as it did so well with the speaker putting his "ear to his cold, wet/skin," which is a wonderful image. Ed also managed to continue by hearing and, later, by looking (and being looked at!).

Renee DeHart, a fourth-grade writer, also uses the senses to continue in her poem, "Sailing":

Sailing

Sailing in my light
blue sailboat,
I hear the white waves
prancing and dancing
across the side
of the little boat.
The stars sing
a short, beautiful lullaby
as I lie,
my eyes deep in thought.
The moonlight sprays
on the silent
sandy beach.
The sail looks like
a blanket swaying
on the gentle breeze,
as my shoelaces dance
up and down my feet
in a lovely rhythm.

****

The great pleasure of this poem for me is not in its sense-continuations, but in its last few lines, with the dance of the shoelaces; however, Renee probably would not have gotten to those last few lines if she had not used the senses to continue.

A poem that more directly uses the senses to continue is "Mr. Grasshopper," by Abby McKellin, a fourth-grade writer:

Mr. Grasshopper

Hiding by
      the cucumbers,
he looks like
        a neon green
  leaf.
     Watching him
you think
       of a dew drop
falling off
       a birch tree.
Touching him
      makes you feel
special
      like you were
   dancing
     on a
rose petal,
      while
 a red butterfly
    glides by
and Mr. Grasshopper follows
    behind
like the whispering wind.

    ****

Continuing through Repetition of a Specific Word or Phrase

A third technique that may help the beginning writer to continue is the repetition of specific words and phrases.

Word Repetition

The word may be the name of a person, place, or thing, such as Han Shan, Broad Street, or diamond, which is repeated at certain intervals during the poem in order to continue the established rhythm. For instance, if the writer gets stuck, the repetition of Han Shan's name may very well help him or her to conjure up another detail for the poem; the same is true for Broad Street or diamond. This repetition does not have to form a strict pattern. It may be random, and in fact probably will be, since its purpose is to provide a new breath to the writer only when needed.

"Han Shan," a poem of direct address by Lisa Ryan, a sixth-grade writer, uses repetition of the name to continue:

Han Shan

Han Shan, I found you,
you cannot hide from me.

Han Shan, what is silence to you?

Is silence like a leaf
    drifting down
    from cloudy skies?
Or is it like a rainbow
    springing from
    the plain dry earth?

Han Shan, tell me,

    is the wind wild
    and free,
    or just a breeze?

Tell me, Han Shan, tell me.

     ****

In addition to the repetition of the name, Han Shan, in this poem, Lisa also creates strong parallel structure in stanza three, a structure which is reinforced by the repetition of the name in each stanza.

The repetition of a color also may provide the writer with momentum, as is seen in "Green," by Erin Brady, a third-grade student.

Green

Sitting in the green field
with green as far as the eye can see
except for the blue of the sky and white of the clouds,
like we are lost in a world of green
wondering where the greenness ends.

     ****

Phrase Repetition

The repetition of a phrase also helps the writer to continue writing by providing a rhythmical base from which to begin again. I have found repetition of phrases to be even more helpful than repetition of words, probably because of the more definite rhythm that is established with the phrase. Although the beginning writers may not be able to express what the rhythm is in terms of stressed and unstressed syllables, they will usually hear the rhythmical patterns, patterns which set up certain rhythmical expectations the writers may then decide to fulfill or not. (For a more detailed discussion of phrase repetition, please see *Chapter Thirteen, FIRST LINE/RHYTHM POEM.*)

"Black Yellow," by Jennifer Dyer, a seventh-grade writer, uses repetition of the phrase, "Back in the night when I was born" to continue writing, and that repetition also creates the repetition of black yellow which in turn unifies the poem and propels its words.

Black Yellow

Back in the night
when I was born
I heard honking taxis --
black
yellow
checkered
in the bustling city.
Back in the night
when I was born
my mind
was full
of questions
like the nest
was full of hornets --
black
yellow
striped
resting on the limb
of the shrub.
Back in the night
when I was born
I felt my mother
trembling
like the desert surface
after the cheetahs --
black
yellow
spotted
stampeded by.
Back in the night
when I was born

we looked down
at the sky --
black
yellow
twinkling
in the heavens
before I came to earth.

      ****

One of my favorite repetition exercises to use with junior high or high school students is what I call the "Let the rain kiss" exercise, an idea which I got from Langston Hughes' wonderful poem, "April Rain Song," which is also discussed more fully in *Chapter Thirteen, FIRST-LINE POEM.*

As an example of how such repetition can help a student to continue writing, I've excerpted a section from a long poem by Sonasha Braxton, an eighth-grade writer:

Let the Rain Kiss

Let the rain kiss
the starving children in Bosnia
their thirst is great
Let the rain kiss
the trash cans
in the dark alley...
Let the rain kiss
the father
the mother
the son
the daughter
for they have no place to go
Let the rain drown
the racism
the discrimination
the hatred
the prejudice
and let them flow
into the cleansed waters
so they also
can become cleaned...
Let the rain kiss
the six year old
in the small apartment
who has nightmares
about where her father
is now....

****

All writers, beginners or not, often get stuck at some point in their writing, but some of these techniques may help them to break through such blockage and to continue putting the words down on the page.

CHAPTER SEVEN: HOW TO END

HOW TO END

How, or when, to end a poem is a difficult problem for both beginning and experienced writers alike, for there is no one set way to conclude a poem. Ideally, a poem will end itself, naturally, without calling undue attention to the fact that it is ending. But if this doesn't happen, the following guidelines may help.

Avoid General, "Summary" Endings

First of all, convince the beginning writers that their poems should not become too general, or too abstract, at the end. This tendency to conclude with an abstraction stems from "summary" conclusions many students use to end their essays. Carrying this tendency over into their poetry writing, many beginning writers end their poems weakly by saying something like, "And then I woke from the dream," "It was a wonderful time," or "It made me sad."

End with Sensory Images, Comparisons, Surprising Statements, or Words that Echo a Dominant Sound of the Poem

To counteract this generalizing tendency, ask them to end their poems with sensory images, comparisons, surprising statements, or words that echo a dominant sound of the poem--or a combination of these.

End with a Sensory Image

A poem that ends with a sensory image will anchor the poem in its reality, thus avoiding a generalized conclusion that moves the reader away from the poem rather than back into it. For instance, if the poem is about a man building a house, the last line(s) might contain the sensory detail of the man pounding the last nail into a board, or it might show the man closing the door which he has just set into its frame. Or, if the poem is about a person who is angry in a kitchen, the last lines may be about that person knocking pans off the shelf. And so on.

These poems end effectively with sensory details:

The Lovely Girl

I sit here with the wind
blowing like my heart
beating fast.
My hair shines like a red rose
sitting lonely in a meadow
while small mice scurry
over my black shoes.

   --Kim Hartsock, third grade

     ****

Church

I remember being in church
Sitting in front of the old man in the red suit
As the preacher preached from behind the gold pedestal

I remember walking up to the stone table
And lighting the flowery incense
As the sun's rays sparkled through the stained glass windows
Lighting up the church in extreme reds and yellows

I remember the closing of the coffin
As the mourners said their last prayers
And walked silently from the church.

   --Matthew Sisler, eighth grade

    ****

End with a Comparison

Sometimes the student may end the poem with an apt comparison. This is more difficult than ending with an image, but if the comparison is appropriate, it can be very effective. Billy Dougherty, a fifth-grade writer, ends his poem with a terrific and poetically appropriate comparison:

Han Shan

Han Shan, Han Shan, on top
of Cold Mountain,
as cold as ice,
drinking your wine
like crystal,
drinking alone
yet not alone,
sitting there with your shadow,
like an ocean waving
and whirling,
eating your bark and
leaves, berries and roots,
writing your poems
by moonlight
as bright as 500
flashlights!

    ****

The brilliant light that Billy's comparison brings into the poem is a wonderful image that "lights up" what had seemed to be a "dark" poem..

Kim Donchez, a fourth-grade writer, also uses a delightful comparison to end her little poem:

Book

The quietest moment of my life
is when I'm reading
at the shore,
the waves
moving back and forth,
like pages of the book!

      ****

End with a Surprising Image or Idea

A third way to end a poem is by using a surprising yet somehow appropriate image or idea. Justine Enders, a seventh-grade writer, ends with such a surprise, one that re-echoes and amplifies the poem's meaning:

Lilies of Life

Right now I'm sitting here
in my broken down cottage, in the living room.
My silver colt 4

        5 in my H
           A
           N
           D
Thinking it over.
        I don't know about it.
Is my l   really that bad?
   i
    f
   e

Do I want to let my white lilies wilt,
or am I gonna be here to irrigate my field?

      ****

Here is another example of an ending that is surprising yet wonderfully, poetically appropriate:

Young Girl Cooking

Standing here
by the wooden table,
the white tablecloth
looking like ground-covered snow,
stirring and pouring,
like a machine at work,
I am a young girl
with hair that looks like silk
and an orchestra sounding in my ear.

   --Karin Saminack, fifth grade

     ****

End with a Musical Click

The fourth and final way to end a poem that will be discussed here is what I call the musical "click" poem. As William Butler Yeats, the great Irish poet, once said, a poem should end the way a finely made jewelry box closes, with a "click." That click may be provided musically by echoing a dominant sound of the poem somewhere in the last line, if not in the last word. This musical echo will click the poem shut just as tightly as Yeats's jewelry box closes.

"Farewell," a poem by Mark von Oven, a seventh-grade writer, illustrates such a musical closure:

Farewell

  Listening to the music
I remember the purple church,
  my grandfather lying peacefully
in his glazed oak coffin.
  Taken from never-ending pain
and suffering, sickness and problems,
  they carried him to his grave
as I placed purple roses on top
      and
        quietly
          sobbed.

     ****

The end-word, *sobbed,* strongly echoes the word *top* at the end of line eight, an echo which helps to close the poem with musical finality.

Another example of such musical ending is seen in "The Blue Night," by Ann Gabriel, a sixth-grade writer. Ann's poem is different from Mark's, however, in that she ends with an echo of the strong long *i* vowel sound that dominates the entire poem.

The Blue Night

   When I was a child
I would
     fall in a lake

  like ice cold
  jello gelatin,
tingling in a bright
  blue bowl.
     And I got
  the pneumonia
  and I coughed
like a horse neighing
  at midnight
   in the bright
moonlight shining
  down on a glittering,
red rose flickering in my
      blue eyes,
      that's how I
  remember it.

     ****

The long *i* vowel sound dominates the poem, especially in the second half, and it's appropriate that the second-last line of the poem ends with the *I* as the last stressed syllable, with the last line merely trailing off after it.

There are many ways to end a poem but, as a general rule of thumb, endings should stem naturally from the poem, and they should not be general or abstract summaries (at least not for the beginning writer). They may be surprising yet appropriate, they may either hurl the reader out of the poem (as comparisons usually do), or sink the reader deeper into the poem (as an image usually does), and they may end musically, with an echo of a sound in the last word or line that echoes a previous, dominant sound. If the student has difficulty ending a poem, these techniques may help.

PART THREE: SEQUENCED EXERCISES FOR THE WRITING OF POEMS

CHAPTER EIGHT: VISUALS POEMS

VISUALS POEMS

Using a visual to get students to write can be a very successful exercise, especially since many of the images for the poem are right there for the writer to claim. Because it is an excellent way to help the beginning writers practice their image usage, I like to make this one of my first full-class exercises after introducing the basic concepts of poetry writing.

Postcards, poster-prints, slides, or other visuals may be used, depending upon the class situation. I prefer using prints because I can display several simultaneously (in contrast to using a slide), and students may use images from all of them, thus enhancing poetic juxtapositions. On the other hand, using a slide has the advantages of keeping the students in their seats as well as presenting the images in a bold, dramatic manner. Since I primarily use prints, most of this chapter will be about such usage, but whatever is said may be applied to any type of visual.

Prints

The prints should have a variety of forms and contents, some having human characters in them, some not, some being naturalistic, some being impressionistic or expressionistic, some with action, some with still-lifes, some portraying urban scenes, some rural scenes, and so on. (This variety is discussed more fully later in this chapter).

I like to use at least four prints for the exercise, encouraging the students to draw their images from one or more, as they wish; such variety helps the students because they may not be able to "connect" with just one selected print. Placing the prints at the front of the room, I ask the beginning writers to come up with a pencil and pad of paper, to look carefully at the prints, and to jot down any images that strike them. At this point, I encourage them to become part of the print, perhaps by being the young boy or girl portrayed, the mother, the sailor, or perhaps by being the waves, the oak tree, the bluebird. This immersion into the print is an important step, for once they do this they can see, hear, feel, taste and smell what's going on around them clearly, as the example poems will demonstrate. I put these senses on the board, for the students to refer to, as well as the words think and imagine, and, again, encourage them to use the words when needed.

Use Imagined as Well as Actual Images

Once the students are back in their seats, I'll ask what images they saw in the print(s) that they might use in their poems, and, as they call them out, I put several on the board. If the images are too realistic, I suggest that they imagine other sensory images in the print, or I ask what their character or object thinks, to counteract the tendency to be merely descriptive. This soon becomes a game, with the students trying to out-do each other with their observations and imaginings, which is good.

Use Comparisons

Usually the students will start making comparisons at this point, too, especially if they were making comparisons as a warm-up exercise. For instance, one might note the waves slapping against the boat are like white, angry fingers, or another may note that a cardinal looks like a heart in the snowy field, and so on. If they don't make such comparisons, I will ask them to say what such and such an image sounds like first, again trying to break the usual associations, and then move on to the other senses for comparison-making. Such comparisons will allow the students to bring their imaginations into the print, and thus into the poem, making it more than merely a descriptive piece of writing.

When the class is excited about the prints, and the images and comparisons are being called out regularly, I ask the students to become one of the characters or objects in the print, to begin their poem with an "ing" verb form, to use no more than seven words in a line, and to write at least one full side of a sheet of paper. As I say these things, I write some participles on the board that they may use to begin their poems, such as "Sailing," "Walking," "Sitting," and so on. And, as they begin writing, I stress that they can imagine details for their Print Poem that are not in the print, such as creating a blue sun or hearing an orchestra tuning up, letting them know that they are free to create such details as well as to describe them.

Heather Glaal, a fifth-grader, and Monica Sweigard, a fourth-grader, became characters in their respective prints and presented the images very clearly. Both, too, present creative surprises in their poems, with Heather using an unexpected action and Monica using a strong comparison.

American Gothic

Standing here
next to my beloved husband
with the sharp whispering pitchfork
in his trembling hand
I feel like telling him
in his open ear
to look up
at the bluebird
sitting in the big oak tree
standing up so brightly
in the purple sun.

   --Heather Glaal, fifth grade

    ****

Sap

As I was standing in my dining room
pouring a cup of tea,
a drop fell to the edge
of the table.
It's like sap,
beautiful,

76

dripping from a young maple tree,
so thick,
slowly falling,
like a bead hanging
from a thin piece of string.

   --Monica Sweigard, fourth grade

         ****

Variation: Tell What the Artist Senses

Another approach to the Print Poem is to have the beginning writers describe what they think the artist sensed when he or she created the painting. Peter Hagemeyer, a fifth-grade student, tells us what Vincent Van Gogh heard when painting "Starry Night":

After Starry Night

Vincent Van Gogh
   heard
the breeze
flowing through
the gold grass and leaves,
like the steeple singing free
with all its bells
as the people shine
like diamonds in the sky
on a Starry Night.

         ****

Variation: Use at Least Two Colors

The gold and diamonds in Peter's poem are strong visual images from the painting, sensory impressions which give the poem a colorful texture. To emphasize the color of some paintings in their poems, I'll ask students to mention at least two colors and, if possible, to make the colors dominant in the poem through repetition or placement (usually at the ends of lines).

Jennifer Ring, an eighth-grade writer, emphasizes color in her painting-poem by repeating yellow and blue at the beginning and end.

My Yellow Cockatiel

My yellow cockatiel
by the blue wall
sits on its perch

chirping away,
waking us up
to the morning shade
with loud, cheerful song.
That's my yellow cockatiel
by the blue wall.

****

Lea Librick, a fifth-grade student, emphasizes colors by naming several in her poem, "Walking Along the Shore Banks":

Walking Along the Shore Banks

Walking along the green river
an old man fishes
while a lady picks yellow marigolds
and the wind whistles among the leaves.
Looking along the shore
I see many people feeding brown
  bread to seagulls
and an old lady hanging her blue wash.
Now hawks soar under the purple sky
  where
it is getting late
and dusk is coming
like a pink comet.

****

Variation: Use a Word that Conveys Emotion

Yet another approach to the Print Poem is to ask the students to put a word that conveys a particular emotion into their poems, such as content, careless, or sorrow. This, of all the print exercises, can create surprising effects.

Barb Bergesen, a seventh-grade writer, uses the word content in her poem of the same title:

Content

Standing here
looking onto my garden
full of magnolias and
snapdragons
I realize
how content I am,

happier than the sailboats
that drift out into the sea's freeway,
the air fresh with springtime
and the children's laughter
while I hear the singing
praises of a nearby cello.

     ****

"Careless," by Doug Gauck, a fifth-grade student, conveys an enviable carefree attitude in his print poem:

Careless

Lying by the lake,
careless,
watching boats that need power
other than their own
and troubled people
trudging along
barely carrying their weight.

Nothing wrong.

Perfectly content.

Watching a boy walk by
who wishes he were
careless too
like me and my shadow.

     ****

Or, as Brooks Faure, a fourth-grade writer shows, the emotion of sorrow may be dramatically conveyed:

Waiting

I sit by the ocean
I say no words
longing for my husband
who has gone to sea
The ocean is as cold
as an ice cream cone
The land is as white
as an old man's beard

I wait and wait
to get a letter
All it says
is sorrow

****

Variation: Tell a Story about the Print

Sometimes I will tell a story about a print and then ask the students to write about the print, incorporating some of the details of the story into their poem. This can be a very effective way to teach any content area and then to have the students respond in writing. For instance, I talked about St. Jerome's asceticism when presenting the print of him praying in the desert; I mentioned how he often went without food and water for days, how he often left civilization to be alone with God, and how the luxuries of a daily life must have been quite tempting to him. Given this information, and using images from the print, Amy Todd, a fourth-grader, wrote the following poem:

St. Jerome in the Desert

Here I am in this rock filled land,
watching the old cross
with sharp thorns hanging off,
the rocks whispering to each other
like a soft breeze blowing my beard,
a roaring lion at my feet,
and I know God is on my side.
My home in the other land,
far away and lonely,
I can feel watching me
and calling me back,
but I won't go.
I stay on this dirty earth.
I am sorry for my sins.

****

This exercise works well with nearly any character, as the poems in *Chapter Fifteen, Persona Poem,* show.

The last examples of the Print Poem to be presented here demonstrate how the writers often convey, knowingly or not, their inner concerns and cares by identifying fully with a character or object in the print.

The Portrait

Standing here
holding onto my parrot
like a lion with its helpless prey.
If I don't
Mommy will get mad
like a cold dark tornado
closing in around me.
If I get my red suit
dirty or unpressed
the painter will look at me
like I am a newspaper
with the words washed out.
My neck is getting cramped
and feels like a long gray flagpole
without the flag.
Out of the corner of my eye
I see the cats eyeing the birds
like a tempted flea on a furry animal.
But they are trained not to,
I hope.

   --Becca Tilden, fifth grade

      ****

Divorce

A small girl sits quietly
on the kitchen floor.
In her hands
she holds a metal bowl.
All of a sudden
she feels a tenseness grow
inside of her.
With one angry burst
she hears yells.
She silently slips
out of the kitchen,
runs upstairs,
and leaps onto her bed.
She has no understanding
of what is to come.

   --Toni Zelt, fourth grade

My Mother

As she adds a tint of green
to the poplars
in her painting,
she pictures herself
within the scene
standing on the pebbly beach
looking out across the weedy shore.
My father is there
thinking of a red Jaguar
polished and bright
driving through Tennessee.
His tall form gazes
across the muddy river
at the dusty cement block building
protruding from a looming mountainside.
The leaves on the poplars shake violently
as a loud alarm awakens my mother
from her dreaming
to warn that the cake she is baking
is ready
to be taken out of the oven.
It is time to make dinner.
So she will not have the opportunity
to dream
until tomorrow
when she will paint the gray stormy sky.

   --Jenny Casagrande, eighth grade

CHAPTER NINE: PLACE POEMS

PLACE POEMS

This exercise has similarities with the *Visuals Poems* and *How to Begin* chapters, for it emphasizes the need for a specific physical setting for the poem, a place where sensory images are readily available to the beginning writer. This chapter, however, discusses more fully the variety of such places and how their images may be used.

Select a Unique, Special Place

To begin, I ask the students to put themselves in a place, real or imagined, that has (or had) some strong effect, positive or negative, on them, a place that is somehow special. It is all-important that the place somehow be unique, that the writers make it unique through vivid description and imagining. For instance, if the students are in a tree house, they may watch the maple leaves fall like red and yellow musical notes, or if they are sledding down a blue hill, they might hear the orchestra of the stars in the winter sky, and so on. The mixture of the specific place and the students' imaginings will create an exciting poem that fuses the real and imaginary worlds.

The more unique the place, the better, for their responses will tend to be more unique and original, and thus less cliched. For instance, lying down in a sleeping bag on a camping trip is probably a better setting for a place poem than lying down in a bedroom, since the former setting is a bit unusual and will tend to present more unique images and ideas.

The beginning writers, of course, may select a usual place such as their bedrooms as their special places, as long as they somehow imaginatively make their poem unique and interesting. (Thus the set-up of a Place Poem is very important, for the students will have to work harder to create good poems if they select a place that tends toward cliched images and ideas.) If they want to be in their bedrooms, I suggest they may go under their beds and write the poem from that new perspective. Or if the students wish to be in church, I ask them to see something that no other church member would see, perhaps a stained-glass saint raising a gloved hand to the sun, or the choir music wafting like a rainbow above the altar.

As they name their places, I put them on the board, encouraging them, as always, to "borrow" whatever image might attract them and start them writing. If the places are too usual, I try to guide them to more original ones, which may be done sometimes simply by changing the time of day or season when the speaker is there. The church at midnight, for instance, might be more compelling than the church at 10 a.m. on a Sunday, just as being by a blue pond in winter rather than in spring may create a more unusual and unexpected perspective.

Use the Five Senses

I also ask them what they see, hear, touch, taste, smell, think and imagine in their special places, suggesting that they might eat the leaves from their tree house, leaves that taste like what? Does anyone else go there? Why? What does the sun feel like there? The moon? What do they dream there? And so on. I again encourage the beginning writers to use comparisons as they call out their images, so the wind there may sound like diamonds whispering or dripping water

may sound like roses blooming. Once the students are responding enthusiastically, I ask them to "put themselves"
in their special place, closing their eyes if that helps, and to write.

Raena Latina, a ninth-grade writer, uses vivid images in her place poem:

On the Fire Escape

Sitting on the fire escape
my shirt is matted to my back
as the wind blows
bringing with it the melancholy notes of a saxophone
from a nearby club
and a pink neon sign flashes
GIRLS GIRLS GIRLS
and the TV downstairs drones a Coca-Cola commercial
and steam comes out of the manholes
and glass breaks next to the metal trash bins in the alley
and a woman laughs
and the subway rattles far beneath me
while a lone droplet of sweat forms a path from my hairline
    past my eyebrow
and into my eye
where it stings and I blink
and disturb the stillness.

        ****

Theresa Hegel, a fourth-grader, finds her special place to be in the weeds:

The Weeds

  Sitting in the weeds
  in the summer noon
    I can feel a soft
gentle breeze flowing by.

I see some black termites
  sitting and listening
as the leader gives out orders.

  From far off
 I hear someone
 whispering out words
from a good book in Arizona,

     and the daisies
  singing a sad story
     as the winds
vibrate messages through
    the soft summer leaves

while somewhere in New Jersey
    I hear my grandmother
          baking
    my favorite chocolate chip
          cookies,

making me think just like an
     encyclopedia
until I'm lullabyed to sleep.

         ****

Kamella Miller, an eighth-grade student, saw her special place as a street when a snowstorm began, a time when something extraordinary happened to her:

Dancing in the Snow

Walking home at night
after the wrestling match,
I hear no sound, no cars,
no people.
There is complete
silence, only
the freezing wind scratching
my delicate face.
Then a snowflake, then
  another.
I'm not alone.
As I dance in the snow
I think about being one
  of them.
Quiet, but not still.
Melting on the ground
until I disappear.

         ****

Jonathan Ozimak, a fifth-grade writer, places himself in a natural setting where a special moment also occurs:

The Beach

Sitting on the beach
I see
a fisherman in a red suit
and a green hat
and big black boots.
I smell the sand
like a fireball in the sun.
Suddenly
a cable spool
drifts from a sunken ship
and my father and I
take it home
like a secret.

****

Variation: Try an Urban Scene

Because many older students don't tend to put themselves in a natural setting, such as beside a pond or in tall grasses, I ask them to walk down a main street or an alley in their town, registering whatever sensory details they perceive, especially those of sight and sound. Before writing, I'll ask them for specific images from their various "walks," putting them on the board as they're noted. I encourage them to use those daily images so often overlooked, such as the old man in a wheelchair who sits outside the Army & Navy Store, or the parking meter policewoman who diligently writes out her tickets, assuring them that the litter in the streets is as poetic as a rose in the garden. The students often think such sordid, ordinary images do not belong in poems, but I try to convince them that such images are indeed the core of much contemporary American poetry, reading them Louis Simpson's short, famous poem about American poetry for support:

American Poetry

Whatever it is, it must have
A stomach that can digest
Rubber, coal, uranium, moons, poems.

Like the shark, it contains a shoe.
It must swim for miles through the desert
Uttering cries that are almost human.

****

If they still seem unconvinced, I will read William Carlos Williams' poem, "Between the Walls of the Contagious Hospital," which illustrates how the seemingly sordid may indeed be beautiful. (See *Chapter Thirteen, First Line/Rhythm Poems*, for Dr. Williams' poem.)

Once they understand this concept, that the ordinary may be fabulous and beautiful, they call out details faster than I can write them on the board. When they get to the point of giving full-line details, I ask them to write. (Another beneficial aspect of this exercise is that it helps to create a sense of community among the students, for they are writing about their main street, their town, their lives.)

Kris Aul, a ninth-grader, captures the desperation of his "special" place in his poem:

Chillin' on a park bench off Sarah St.

    Some do at 12th street park.
     We chill by the phone,
      me and the girls,
      smokin' cigarettes
    trying to get it in later.

  5.0 rolls up just to check on us.
    Pager to pager blowin' up,
    telephone ringin' off the hook.

The lowlife boys gather on the hoop court for a game of tips

    others push on the corner.
    A fight breaks out on the court,
  the guys from KOPY's cheer them on.

On a day-to-day basis this stuff happens.
Tomorrow with no doubt this will all happen again.

    ****

Joe Perry, another ninth grade writer, captures the same despondent atmosphere in an haiku-like poem:

  My Street

  Hear gun shots and systems
  The smell of blunts in the air
  Cars burning rubber because they
    Just got somebody.

    ****

The next three Place Poems are from high school students who live in Tamaqua, an old coal-mining town in northeast Pennsylvania. As the poems demonstrate, the Place Poem can be a great vehicle for self expression.

Tamaqua

cold railroad tracks cutting into smoldering streets
step around the broken board
I watch the seltzer bottles and the gray poodles
the trucks spit poison into their faces
abandoned playgrounds with chipped yellow
and chain link fences & sand & weeds
open porch screen doors
bring air to the speckled linoleum and
olive shag carpets.
cycle of motion.
hair blows out windows and
shrieks get lost in the wind
leaving still dry air behind
going away -- 1/2 off sale
shoes in pairs
battered Winnie the Poo poster
exploded in a pile of dust.
smoke clouds in rings
the pink neon lights flash
and the stale bricks
are shingled over year after year.
I pass the overflowing yards of mint
sprinkler left on
gloves facedown in the dried rain
beehives left over --
polyester for Sunday best
plastic stapled on dusty windows
forgotten shadows stand on street corner --
curtains blow in the rain.

    -- Tara Poncavage, eleventh grade

      ****

Broad Street

Cruising down Broad Street
I smell designer imposters
they clot on the corner

encased in a nicotine fog.
Blondes from a bottle, taunting.
Where's your hairspray?
Your hair is ugly & flat,
where's your tight skirt?
You don't wear Spandex?
What kind of music is that?
And look at those shoes
you are so queer!
Louder, louder, louder
and then the green light,
future,
blinks in a blurred flash.

   --Ann Barth, twelfth grade

     ****

Cruising down Broad Street

Cruising down Broad Street,
  listening to "House of Pain,"
I see Howie spray painting
  "Welcome to the Jungle"
while having a flashback of Vietnam.

The old guy with hanging skin
  struts, disturbedly weaving
  between parking meters,
mumbling, growling, "Do you wanna
  start!"
The Motorheads behind Burger King
  screaming and yelling to all the girls,
all have the same rust-colored
  satin jackets,
"The Street-Machine Association."

Nothing to do, nowhere to go,
  the benches across from Piercinni's
are packed every night.
  Why am I here? Where am I going?

I can hear my mother saying
  "Be good, behave yourself, Joanne."
Does she know, I'm still the same.
  Times of change are here now,

Nothing will stop them.

"I'll be home soon, Mom,"
   my mind screams,
black clouds of exhaust fill
   my car as a truck
   buckles into gear.

They tell me the suicide rate of teenagers
in this county I live in is the highest
of the state.
   Give us something to do,
   Some goals of who & what to be.

I turn the car off. Home.
The sweet smell of honeysuckle
   fills my nose,
the whipporwill sings his fairy tales.

   --Joannie Ritter, eleventh grade

For other examples of Place Poems in other natural settings, such as Beach Poems, please see *Chapter Nineteen: Nature Poems*.

CHAPTER TEN: QUIET POEMS

QUIET POEMS

After the students have practiced their image making in their *Visuals* and *Place Poems*, I like to use the *Quiet Poem*, so they can fine tune their hearing abilities. The first step is to find a special place in which their listening can occur, a place that will provide them with readily accessible images from most if not all of the senses. This place should be somehow special, too, such as in a blue rowboat at dawn when the speaker caught his biggest fish, or staring at a yellow wreath in a funeral parlor during a wake for the speaker's grandfather, or perhaps simply walking down a dusty alley at dusk when the speaker sees a piece of broken green glass shimmering like an emerald.

I often suggest the place might be associated, generally, with a moment of great joy, sadness, beauty, accomplishment, and so on; a place and time in which everything grows silent and the speaker feels as though he or she is in another world.

Hear Both Imagined and Actual Sounds

As the students call out their special places, I write them on the board, again encouraging all the writers to use whatever place that might propel their poems. If a student suggests a church as a quiet place, I'll ask what he or she hears there, emphasizing that the sounds do not have to be realistic, but that many of them should indeed be imagined.

So if a student says one sound is the creak of the pew, I might ask if the stone angel on the altar is whispering to anyone in the church--to give them an example of the kind of imagining that may occur in the poem. The students quickly warm to this kind of listening and the board is soon filled with real and imagined sounds of various special places.

If the students aren't listening well, I sometimes ask them to close their eyes and I'll make a noise, perhaps by clinking my keys or by tapping the blackboard with a ruler, asking them what that sound sounds like. This usually helps to get them into the listening groove.

Then I start asking what the sounds they hear are like, again encouraging strong and unusual comparisons; for instance, the stone angels whispering might sound like a black rose dropping its petals, or like an old lady slowly stepping down the aisle, and so on. Such comparison making will allow the beginning writers the imaginative freedom they need in order to create original and authentic poems.

Then We Write

Now they are ready to write. Again, to help the students put themselves directly into the experience, I put several "ing" verb forms, participles, on the board, such as *Walking, Listening, Standing, Sailing* and so on. I also point out that they should first hear something, but that they should also use the other senses (which are written on the board) too. After reminding them to keep their lines short, and that they should complete at least one full page of writing, we begin. Louise Romano, a fifth grade writer, listens well in her poem, "As I Listen":

As I Listen

Sitting
  on the porch
  of the old broken
     down house,
    I strain to hear
red robins
      yanking
    earth worms
from the moist earth.
    The air
       blows gently
    and in the distance
     I can hear
  a dance of white
       butterflies,
dandelions releasing
         parachutes,
     soldiers marching
  to the wild beat of their hearts
     until my mother calls.

       ****

Christine Newell, a sixth-grade student, puts herself in her bedroom to listen and imagine:

Listening

Sitting on my bedroom floor
  I can hear
     my golden superball
    crack in half
like a red ketchup bottle popping open,
and my sister quietly dancing
    in her yellow flowerbed,
     her show
      suddenly snapping
like an apple being bitten
  in the supermarket.
  And I hear
    my mother
chewing watermelon bubblegum,
throwing the paper away
like a colorful butterfly

quietly fluttering in the moonlight
  while I sit here
    listening
 and hear everything
    drifting...
      drifting...
       drifting...
        into silence.

   ****

Variation: the Quietest Time (or Moment) in My Life

A variation of the listening poem is what I call the *Quietest Time* or the *Quietest Moment in My Life Poem*. This exercise still places the emphasis on listening, but it's about a time and place in the writers' pasts that has, for some reason, remained vivid in their memories.

The first step in this exercise is to ask the writers to remember the quietest moment in their lives, suggesting that it may have been, again, at a time of great joy or sorrow, a time of great beauty or ugliness, or perhaps a time of great contentment. As the students remember such moments, I put them on the board, asking what they heard, then saw, touched, smelled, tasted, thought, felt, et cetera, encouraging them, as before, to imagine as well as to remember. Michelle Swey, a fifth-grade writer, captures this quiet moment well in her poem, "The Quietest Time":

The Quietest Time

The quietest time in my life
is when I go down under my bed,
I just sing softly to myself,

and when I walk to school,
I'm just as quiet as a kitten.

And when I go on the trails
with my friends,
we're as quiet as flowers
growing in the ground.

   ****

Douglas Grietzes, another fifth-grader, has a strong flowing movement in his *Quiet Moment Poem*:

Dad

The quietest moment

97

of my life
was when me
and my Dad
went fishing,
it sounded
like rain drops
splashing
into the water
and
the fish jumping
and the reel like crickets
as the water
was running
downstream.

****

Jeff Krouse, a sixth-grade writer, uses vivid images in his *Quiet Poem*:

Quiet

The quietest moment of my life
is just before I drop to sleep
and I hear the snap of sparks
in the fireplace downstairs.
I hear the bullfrog croaking in the lake,
and the crackling caterpillars
muching heartily on leaves
until they are all gone.
I hear the chirps of crickets
like fiddlers in the night...
all is quiet as a leaf
drifting to the ground,
quiet.

****

Linda Jo Youngkin, a third-grader, captures a special moment in her *Quiet Poem*:

The Quietest Moment

That moment
is when you're
all alone
on an ice rink
practicing

and you think
you are a star
singular
burning bright.

****

Variation: Quiet Means to Me

Yet another variation of this Quiet Poem is what I call the Quiet Means to Me Poem, so the students are not remembering a quiet moment but are instead saying what quiet means to them. Mark Mitman, a fourth-grade writer, has a surprising twist at the end of his poem:

Quiet Means to Me

Quiet means to me
sitting in bed at night
by myself,
hearing cars pass
like ships bumping
through the water
way offshore.
It means standing
in a crowd
with no one
I know.
Quiet means to me
visiting my grandfather's grave
with wind blowing through my hair,
standing there,
talking to myself,
whispering quietly.

****

Jennifer Hager, a fifth-grader, captures the meaning of quiet in her poem of the same title:

Quiet

Quiet means to me
a bright and sunny
Saturday morning in January
after a heavy snow fall
with crystal white snow
covering the ground
and hiding the cars in driveways

and along the streets.
No one is moving,
everything is still
as I look out my bedroom window
down at the glistening snow.

     ****

Variation: "Now, When I Listen Carefully, I Can Hear"

After the students seem to have exhausted the possibilities of the *Quiet Poem*, I will ask them to write another one but, this time, when they think they can no longer hear anything else, to write the sentence, "Now, when I listen carefully, I can hear," and to put down things that people cannot ordinarily hear (or, in other words, to imagine such things). I write the sentence on the board, too, so they won't forget it.

I stress that the students should hear things they normally would not be able to hear, such as their grandfathers' heartbeats as they play cards at the table, or the ants singing a marching song as they climb the bark of the oak tree, or perhaps a church bell thinking about pealing one high note at noon. This is when many of the most imaginative moments of the poem occur; the writers are free to hear anything they want, without the limitations or expectations of logic.

The Willow

In the woods
as silent as a fly,
I saw a willow
as it grew
and grew,
its lovely
arms looked
more and more
like tentacles
turning orange
in the setting
sun. Listening
carefully I heard
the field mice
walking, climbing
wheat stalks thin
as a thread. Soon,
they said, the
willow will
come alive
and dance
soft as a cloud

in any wind.

--Melissa Tavares, fourth grade

****

Sorrow to Beauty

Standing by my father's grave, I hear
 my mother weeping
 as I watch a single tear
 ripple down her cheek.

I watch as it plunges down
 on a passing ladybug
 kerplunk!

I listen carefully and hear
 my father's whisper
 like a cold winter breeze
 passing through an old abandoned house.

Suddenly I hear a caterpillar
 crawling through tall grass
 like a child lost in a department store.

With a deep sigh, I think that
 soon the caterpillar
 will show its beauty
 and spread its wings
 to take flight
 to a distant land.

--Maureen Dougherty, ninth grade

****

Then, usually, a student will take the exercise and make it his or her own, as Meg McLaughlin, a sixth-grade writer does:

Grandfather

Walking through the autumn woods,
we have to take each step slowly,
I feel it might be our last walk
 together.

These woods always remind me
    of him,
all the trees slowly dying,
turning brown instead of green.
I have to talk loudly so he can hear me,
    my voice
echoes through the whole forest,
a sad time for me.
The sun rays come down
    still
setting all the leaves on fire
with bright orange
    and red.

CHAPTER ELEVEN: SILENT SPIDER POEMS

SILENT SPIDER POEMS

The *Silent Spider Poem* is a spin-off of the *Quiet Poem* exercise, with the same emphasis on listening, but this time the students can imaginatively leave themselves behind as they either follow the spider or become the spider. One benefit of this exercise is that the students usually connect immediately with the silence of the spider and they enjoy trying to be as quiet as he is as they follow or become him. Such quietness encourages the beginning writers to listen very carefully, as well as to change their perspectives from human beings to arachnids, and thus provides them with images and thoughts they probably would not have obtained otherwise.

Talk about the Spider

I like to use this exercise after the *Quiet Poem* writing, so the students are used to listening and comparing what they hear to other, unexpected things. Before writing, however, I talk about spiders with the students, asking them how large the spider's eyes are, how many legs it has, how it produces its threads, why their webs have designs, et cetera. As interesting details are mentioned, I put them on the board, a favorite of many students being that the spider produces its own silky threads in its body.

Put the Spider in a Special Place

Once the students have enough information about the spider, I ask them to put their spider in a special place, one which will provide plenty of sensory images so the spider can see, hear, touch (with all eight legs!), taste and smell as it journeys. Some will place the spider in the classroom, so we name some of the interesting images there, such as the paper violets or the whirling blue globe, or perhaps the titles of math and spelling books. Others will place the spider in a garden, with its plump tomatoes and long leeks, its sunflowers and compost. Wherever the students place the spider, I stress that they use the specific images of that place, as well as their own imaginings.

Then I suggest that the students may either follow and hear the spider, or that they may be the spider, both alternatives freeing the writers to imagine as well as objectively describe. Kelly Prall, a sixth grade writer, ends her delightful *Spider Poem* with a wonderful comparison:

The Silent Spider

Hiding among my cucumber vines
I hear the spider
   silent
as wisps of cream
melting into coffee.
He waddles slowly, like a duck
over my rosy tomatoes,
over the bean plants,
across the rows.
He struggles over the plum-colored eggplants,

over the picket fence.
I follow, trying to be
as silent as he.
Over a fern leaf,
over a gopher's moist, cool nose,
    I follow,
over a daisy, onto his home,
like a hammock swiftly spun between
      two roses,
         delicate,
            soft,
               silent.

****

Being the Spider

John Blazeck, a fourth grade writer, becomes the spider and wonders about some very interesting ideas in lines that seem to mirror the spider's strings of thread:

I the Spider

I the spider
  feel
    the wind blowing
      as a
        dangling
          string
    holds me from
        falling
        into
          a deep blue sea
          of roses.
And I the Spider
  wonder
    how Time
      gets trapped
      in my silver web
    and how does a
      heart
    stay red.

****

Variation: Using the Five Senses

Another approach to the *Spider Poem*, whether listening or being the spider, is by using some or all of the five senses, as Emily Caffee, a fourth-grade writer, does:

I the Spider

Listen to the light in the forest
     Dance
  behind
     the willow tree,
Watch
   the children
     from behind
the globe in
      the
        classroom.
I
 Touch
   the
    heart
      of the light
    and
   play
    behind
    the newspaper scrap
  until
    Time
      disappears.

    ****

Variation: the Spider Comparison

Or the *Spider Poem* may result simply and directly in one effective comparison, as in "The Silent Creature," by Derek Heppe, a sixth-grader:

The Silent Creature

A spider
  is as
   silent
    as a

small
  white
   tissue
    slowly

dropping
  from a
    maroon coffee
      table

  in the center
    of
    the
    town
    hall.

****

And, again, there is the imaginative hybrid that some students wonderfully create, this one illustrating how the writer first follows and then, in a way, becomes the spider:

The Collapsing Spider

  Kneeling in my flower shop
I listen to the silent spider
  as a star shoots across
  the midst of darkness.
    Creeping, crawling, up my sneaker,
to my arm, then my neck, it reached
    my head,
      then into my brain.

  It shoots out a string of glistening
      silk
to the poppies, then sneaks over to
the pansies, shoots once more into a bucket
  of fresh dirt, tumbles and releases
    its young
before it dies, folding like a flag being
  brought down after a war.

  --Stephanie Gitler, sixth grade

****

The *Silent Spider Poem* is great fun for the beginning writers, especially if they have a special place filled with images for the spider to see, hear, touch, smell and taste.

CHAPTER TWELVE: LETTER POEMS

LETTER POEMS

Letter poems are good exercises in which the beginning writers may use a time-honored literary form to convey their thoughts and feelings. From Ovid to Richard Hugo, poets have used letter poems to directly address another person or the reader, thus achieving an immediacy of communication not often seen in the other exercise poems.

Letter Poem to Han Shan

Although the poems may address anyone, I ask the students to direct their first letter poems to a great, ancient Chinese poet, Han Shan, who lived during the T'ang Dynasty and who has the pseudonym of Cold Mountain. We use Han Shan because he is a distant and rather exotic figure, someone who did not care for material goods at all and lived a reclusive life in the mountains, writing poems. Students are attracted to the strangeness of Han Shan, how he was non-materialistic, how he did not lead a "normal" life, and how he suffered severe hardships to do what he wanted to do: write poems.

Han Shan's distance in time and space also frees the students of self-censoring restraints, and they write their poems to him with an amazing candor and directness.

Talk about Ancient China

In order to write well about Han Shan, however, the students must have images to refer to, sensory details from his life that they may use in their poems. Therefore, I always talk about the time period in which Han Shan lived, sometimes making up details as I go that are not historically true, discussing the jade lions that often guarded rich people's houses in ancient China, the dragons they revered, the chrysanthemums that so often appear in Chinese poems, as well as any other images that might come to mind. (I also put poster prints of Chinese scenes up, encouraging the students to use any images they find motivating.)

Talk about Han Shan

In addition to generally discussing Chinese culture and customs, I also tell them a (sometimes fabricated) story about Han Shan, usually how he had a wife and children, a good job for the Emperor, and how, one day, he woke up and realized he was not happy with his life, and so he left it all to go to Cold Mountain to write poems. The fact that he would leave his family behind arouses strong reactions in some of the students, and those reactions find strong words in their poems (as seen in some of the examples). Once the students and I are there on Cold Mountain with Han Shan, enduring the snow which fell half the year, I ask them what he ate and drank, who his friends were, how he kept himself warm, who he talked to, and so on. In this way, the students begin thinking of Han Shan's physical, as well as emotional and spiritual, existence and they begin to see him as a living, human being and they address him as such in their poems.

As the students mention images of Han Shan's life, I write them on the board, with some of those I've already mentioned, encouraging the students to use whatever they find powerful and propelling. And, as we put the images on the board, I will ask for comparisons; for example, what does the red dragon sound like in the night, or how do the chrysanthemum petals fall in cold November? Some or all of these images and comparisons may be used in the poem.

Read and Discuss Han Shan's Poem, "Drinking in the Moonlight"

Then I read Han Shan's famous poem, "Drinking in the Moonlight," asking the students to write down any images, thoughts or feelings that come to them as I read, so they may use them in their poems.

Drinking in the Moonlight

I sit with my wine jar
among flowers
blossoming trees

no one to drink with

well, there's the moon

I raise my cup
and ask him to join me
bringing my shadow
making us three

but the moon doesn't seem to be drinking
and my shadow just creeps around behind me

still, we're companions tonight
me, the moon, and the shadow
we're observing
the rites of spring

I sing
and the moon rocks back and forth
I dance
and my shadow
weaves and tumbles with me

we celebrate for a while
then go our own ways, drunk

may we meet again someday
in the white river of stars
overhead!

   --Han Shan

112

****

Before asking the students to write their letter poem to Han Shan, we discuss the poem briefly. For instance, I might ask if they could improve the second and third lines, perhaps by making them more imagistic, and usually the students will gleefully point out that "flowers" could be chrysanthemums or some other particular flower, and that "trees" could be cherry trees, et cetera. Then I might ask why he's drinking with the moon and his shadow, making sure they understand how alone he is in nature. Another possible question is whether the moon really "rocks back and forth," or if it is only his shadow "that weaves and tumbles," and, again, most students will point out that Han Shan is the one who is rocking and weaving! These kinds of questions get the students immediately involved in the poem and Han Shan's life, at which point we are ready to write.

Then We Write

Encouraging them to keep their lines short (six or seven lines or less, usually), to use specific sensory images as well as imaginings, and to make comparisons, I ask the students to write to Han Shan, telling him what they think of his life, or perhaps asking him questions. The resultant poems show genuine relationships between the writers and Han Shan.

Han Shan Letter Poems

To Han Shan

Dear Han Shan,
how do you write
poems so beautiful?
I can see you right now,
sitting in the moonlight,
    swaying
like a willow
with the wine bottle
clutched in your hands.
You sing to the stars
as bright as the sun,
and they answer you.

  --Lisa Siftar, fifth grade

    ****

Dawn Reagle, a sixth-grade writer, had a much angrier response to Han Shan's life story:

Cruel, Mean Han-Shan

113

It wasn't very nice of you
  to be so
   cruel.
   Of course
maybe your family was glad you left.
You're always as drunk as a fly that sits
  on an elephant trunk,
  drinking your disgusting
   Blue Booze.
 You left your family to
be as poor as feathers falling
   from the
   dark
   gray
   sky.
You know you were lonely,
lonely as the moon in the sky,
  even with your shadow
   and the moon
   and your poems,
 it was all an ugly lie!

  ****

Erin Coats, a ninth-grade student, had a more aesthetic response, actually having Han Shan create a poem within his poem:

Dear Han Shan,

I see you with your long, skinny black braid down the middle
 of your back,
squatting in your kimono by the fire.
You're staring at one of the pitch-black stones, a blue wine
 bottle in hand
which spills on the blossoming flower of your red robe,
startling you, making you jump up, brush against the flames,
setting yourself on fire.
As you run to the stream that carries your obsession, you
 think of a poem.
It goes something like this:

The sun is always shining here,
It never leaves my spirit.
I may be alone, separated from human life,
Yet I have friends,
The Sun,

114

The Moon,
My Shadow.
And best of all, most compatible,
Born to live with me and each other,
My pen and paper.
They hold my reason for love and life.
Without them I would die.

Han Shan
    you do not stand with the chorus anymore,
yet you sing a soliloquy that no one else can own.

Sincerely,

Your Accompanist,

Erin Coats

     ****

Variation: Han Shan Letter/Print Poems

A variation of this exercise, as mentioned earlier, is using one or more prints with Chinese images that the students may "borrow" as they write. For the class in which the following poems were written, I used a print of white geese drifting down a black river in winter, with ice and snow on the banks; another print displayed a gold dragon shooting flames from its mouth as it soared through a dark blue sky.

Dear Han Shan

I feel your sadness
  floating swiftly down
the cold shallow river like
  the quiet white geese,

I see your soul escaping out
  of the bright orange carp
as the great blue heron snatches
  his last cold meal,

I see you sitting by the hot
  black rocks
as the golden dragon peacefully
  flies through
the dark, cold, silk night.

****

The Ones You Left Behind

Han Shan,

   Hiding in your shell

of your soul

floating slowly away

petals drifting slowly

as the night approaches

like the dragon's wings

through twilight while

do you ever think about

do you hear the tears

unceasingly

casting your life into the sea

losing yourself

like the cherry blossom

through the sky

a dark cloak

silently soaring

I secretly wonder

those you left behind

rolling onto the wings

of the white geese?

   --Crystal Hardelong, eighth grade

****

Variation: General Letter Poem

A more general variation of this "Dear Han Shan" poem is the "Dear _____" poem. Older students, usually from grade six upward, do well with this exercise, sometimes addressing the letter to a parent, an historical figure, a boyfriend or girlfriend, or some other significant person. Before attempting this type of poem, though, it is essential that the writer has a definite memory or set of images to refer to while writing. In other words, they should write, say, to a friend about a black bicycle, or to a mother about a Sunday walk in an amusement park. If they do not locate the
poems in particular places, the poems tend to be very general and abstract.

To counteract this tendency, we talk about the images associated with the person to whom they are writing. For instance, if they write to a grandmother, I ask what that grandmother's favorite

object was -- a gold watch? A 1952 Oldsmobile? Did she rise at five a.m. or sleep till noon?
Did she have a bad heart? And so on. Then we read a few letter poems written by other students
and, when done, write. I include poems written by teachers during this exercise, to illustrate how
the *Letter Poem* can work for people of all ages.

By the River

Dear Mother, I remember
our walk by the river,
listening to the wind whiz
  through
the oak trees while father
fished in the glazing lake.
Snap snap
his line tightened
and a shiny goldfish
was pulled up.
The tulips sensed the air
with a beautiful scent
and the houses stood
as still as a picture
till the river whispered
like a baby's cry
waking us.

    --Renee Gentile, fifth grade

      ****

Dear Grandma

Firewood warmed the room
  Where the front door stood wide
Open. Coffee's steam enveloped
    The morning air.

  Your hands still strong
  Kept the yellow house, set
Back on a Georgian dirt road.
    Plants grew
  Everywhere, some riotous
  And lush, others in neat
    Rows. I remember
  Your chicken coop, the rusted
Wire windows, and how you doctored
    That bird destined to be

Next Sunday's dinner.

The rituals of church
And weekly deliveries from the corner store,
    Ticked away the years.
    You came to Pittsburgh ... Spirit
        Filling a smaller space
        Left shoulders stooped,
        Roots untaken.

    --Lucy Ware, Pittsburgh area teacher

        ****

Note: A famous use of the Letter Poem is William Carlos Williams' "This Is Just to Say," a poem made from a note that Dr. Williams left for his wife, Flossie, after eating some plums he knew she was saving for her breakfast. Because this exercise has been done so often, I do not include any discussion or example poems, but Dr. Williams' poem is printed below:

This Is Just to Say

I have eaten
the plums
that were in
the icebox

and which
you were probably
saving
for breakfast

Forgive me
they were delicious
so sweet
and so cold

        ****

The *Letter Poem* exercise may be addressed to any person, thus allowing a great freedom of choice for the teacher and beginning writers. For instance, if Zapata, the great Mexican revolutionary, is being discussed, why not have the students write a poem to him? Or Einstein? Madame Curie? Hitler? And so on. Just be sure the students know enough about the person, true or not, and they will create lively letter poems.

CHAPTER THIRTEEN: FIRST LINE/RHYTHM POEMS

FIRST LINE/RHYTHM POEMS

This exercise is most successful after students have written *Rose* and *Print Poems*, for in those poems they have become familiar with comparisons and images. Now they are ready for rhythm or prosody, which, generally speaking, deals with the number of stressed and unstressed syllables in a line of poetry, or, in other words, the rhythm of the line. Prosody is a very complex topic, as any good poetry handbook will demonstrate, but a teacher may still use rhythm to motivate writing without spending two weeks defining the term.

Start with a Strong, Rhythmical Line

Start with a phrase or sentence that has a particularly strong rhythm to it; you do not have to count stressed and unstressed syllables, just listen to it. One of several which I have used is "Let the rain kiss," which is taken from Langston Hughes' wonderful poem, "April Rain Song":

April Rain Song

Let the rain kiss you.
Let the rain beat upon your head with silver liquid drops.
Let the rain sing you a lullaby.

The rain makes still pools on the sidewalk.
The rain making running pools in the gutter.
The rain plays a little sleep-song on our roof at night--

And I love the rain.

****

After I read the poem to the class, I put the line, "Let the rain kiss" on the board, and I ask them what kinds of people, places or things their rain might kiss, stressing that their objects can be imaginary as well as real, and that they may be (supposedly) ugly as well as beautiful--reminding them here of William Carlos Williams' poem, "Between Walls," which emphasizes how beautiful the "pieces of a green/bottle" are, even though they lie in cinders "between walls."

Between Walls

the back wings
of the
hospital where
nothing

will grow lie
cinders

in which shine

the broken

pieces of a green
bottle

          ****

Once the students understand they can have their rain kiss anything, they usually become very enthusiastic and call out image after image, which I put on the board with the usual encouragement that they may "borrow" any image that will help their writing. I also try to get them to name images that are parts of their lives, such as the maroon Ford Taurus, the American flag, the bully on the corner, et cetera. Usually the combination of such realistic details with their imaginings produce good, interesting poetic associations.

After we have plenty of images on the board, I talk about the transformative power of rain, how it moistens the earth and helps things to grow, asking them for examples that are real and imagined, stressing that the rain should kiss things other than plants. Then I put a "so" on the second line, just beneath "Let the rain kiss...," and I ask the students to create a poem that follows the same structure, such as,

"Let the rain kiss the hungry,
so they shall have bread in their mouths,"

and so on. If they put down a few such images and run out of words, I encourage them to repeat the line, "Let the rain kiss," with the hope that it will fuel their imaginations and help them to continue writing, as the example poems demonstrate. Then we write.

Tamika Vactor, an eighth-grade student, uses wonderful transformations in her poem:

LET THE RAIN KISS

Teenage mothers with their babies &
Broken beer cans or bottles.

LET THE RAIN KISS
Jesus so He can
Touch Drunk People,
Cigarette butts, Smokers &
Drugs.

LET THE RAIN KISS
12- & 13-year-old girls
So they don't get
Pregnant.

LET THE RAIN KISS

My brother so he
Can get a good
Education.

LET THE RAIN KISS
The Flowers in
Yards,
Lilies & Roses.

LET THE RAIN KISS
My mother so she is
Strong before she dies
Walking
Up three flights of stairs.

LET THE RAIN KISS
My Aunt Avie so she
Can find another job
In Pittsburgh.

LET THE RAIN KISS
Me for when my grandmother dies
I can be strong.

LET THE RAIN KISS
Me so I can go to Medical School.

LET THE RAIN KISS
Bloody Jesus for making people
Believe in themselves.

****

Two of the great benefits of this exercise are that it helps students to break expected associations (through the use of a catalogue, or list of images rather than a narrative), and that it provides students with a way to begin again once their imaginations begin to flag. The refraining line, "Let the rain kiss," provides them with a strong, repeating rhythm that will help them to start all over again, using any new image or idea that pops into their heads. This kind of "popping" is an essential ingredient in good poems, for it allows the writers great imaginative freedom.

To show the real power a beginning writer may get from this exercise, consider the intensity of emotion and vivid imagery in this poem by Sonasha Braxton, an eighth-grade student:

Let the Rain Kiss

Let the rain kiss

the starving children in Bosnia
their hunger is great
Let the rain kiss
the trash cans
in the dark alley
Let the rain kiss
the chairs toppled over
and couches with ripped seams
in front
of my garbage
Let the rain kiss
the small child
abandoned and unwanted
Let the rain kiss
the rooftops
so they bless
the keepers of the house
Let the rain kiss
the ark
in the possession of Noah
Let the rain kiss
the blooming flowers
in the midst of winter
Let the rain kiss
the cross
the barren field
that needs sunlight
Let the rain kiss
the picture of Jesus
hanging on the basement wall
Let the rain kiss
the father
the mother
the son
the daughter
for they have no place to go
Let the rain drown
the racism
the discrimination
the hatred
the prejudice
and let them flow into
the cleansed waters
so they also
can become cleaned
Let the rain kiss

the grass
for it is brown and withered
from drought
Let the rain kiss
the finger puppet
in the decrepit
aging trash can
the puppet no longer
in use
because mother and son
have drifted apart
Let the rain kiss
the old drunk
who staggers up and down
the streets
limping on one leg
the other lost in Vietnam
Let the rain kiss
the six-year-old
in the small apartment
who has nightmares
about where her father
is now
she doesn't quite understand
the meaning of death
Let the rain kiss
the earth
so the flowers
will bloom
life will flourish
anger and hatred will
become happiness
and the world will become
a better place
Let the rain kiss.

****

Variation: "Let the Rain (Powerful Verb)"

One variation uses the same basic phrase, but asks the students to use different, powerful verbs instead of "kiss," as Kira Botkin, a sixth-grade student, does so well in this excerpt from her poem:

Rain

...let the rain grasp
the widow's piano
so it may play joyously again...
let the rain wash
the mist away from
a divorceable couple
so they may see eye to eye again...
let the rain probe
the farmer's fields
so they may never know drought
let the rain pummel
the drug dealers
and fling their merchandise from them....

****

Variation: "Let the Music...."

Another variation of the "Let the Rain Kiss" poem is "Let the Music..," as shown in these few excerpted lines from a poem by Caitlin Jacob, a seventh-grade student:

The Music

Let the music swirl the reds and blues of the fallen tree in
   the forgotten painting
Let the music comfort the uneaten wedding cake
Let the music wash the dirt from the toenails of the lonely
   weeping women
Let the music stop the sweet man from making unimaginable
   mistakes....

****

Variation: "Back in the night when I was born" and "It is Friday":

Any rhythmical line will work for this exercise, so as you read poems, if a line strikes your ear as having a strong rhythm that your students may connect with, try it. A couple that I have tried successfully with younger students are "Back in the night when I was born," and "It is Friday":

Back in the Night

Back in the night when I was born
the moon grew blue
and in the darkness I saw
black shadows of people
standing above me.

Back in the night when I was born
I heard the sounds of voices
talking like the wind pushing
the ocean water.

Back in the night when I was born
I saw the beautiful stars glowing
turquoise and gold,
I heard the clock telling the time
of life.

Back in the night when I was born
I prayed time would be endless
and not be counted like the waves
of the sea floating upon
each other for infinity.

--Roberta Setzer, seventh grade

****

It Is Friday

It is Friday,
Money flows from Dad's tired hands
as he settles into a world
    of velvet,
comforting his back
after a long week at work.

It is Friday,
Children go to a school dance
and enter a galaxy
    of sound,
blasting out the boredom
    of school.

It is Friday,
The world is a deflated balloon
trying to blow itself up,
    trying unsuccessfully,
    again and again.

It is Friday.
The world turns to gold.

--Tracy Grather, sixth grade

****

Variation: "I Have Seen the Best Minds of My Generation"

A line which evokes strong emotions and images from older students is a slight variation of one taken from Allen Ginsberg's "Howl": "I saw the best minds of my generation destroyed by madness, starving hysterical naked,..." I usually convert this to "I have seen the best minds of my generation" and ask the students what they think is happening to their generation. The responses are startlingly powerful, as shown in this poem by Heather Mateyak, a ninth-grade student:

I Have Seen

I have seen the best
minds of my generation
wasted on alcohol and
high on drugs.
I see them on Mauch Chunk Street
and by the Comfort Station.
I see them as they drive to school
and on Piercinni's corner.
I have heard the best
minds of my generation
yelling obscenities
and starting fights.
I hear their lighters
and their beer can tabs.
I see their graffiti
and outened cigarettes.
I hear their deafening music
and old Novas.
I see young mothers with bent heads
and unfeeling fathers telling jokes to buddies.
I hear their babies whimper
and their baby carriages squeak.
I feel their worthlessness,
I feel their loss of dreams.

****

Or the repeating line may not begin the stanzas of the poem, but rather end them, as in this poem by another ninth-grade writer, Daltha Freeman:

Untitled (from an exercise with Len Roberts)

I--Trojan Man

I've seen the best minds of my generation
Get drunk in the basement at a party
Get high in the bathtub
Get screwed in the closet
Get pregnant 'cause of a dare
Get killed by a gunshot
Get buried by their best friends
It sucks to be cool

II--Newport

Bang, Bang
You're dead
You're high
You're drunk
You're hard
You're nothing
It sucks to be cool

III--Jack Daniels

Out of 1500
In a school
20% don't smoke
10% don't screw
5% don't get high
3% don't get drunk
1% don't do anything
But lie in a grave
It sucks to be cool

IV--These are my only friends

All I have to say
To these fools on the street corner
Is
It sucks to be cool
It sucks to be you

****

As is evident from the example poems above, it doesn't matter what phrase or line is used in this exercise, as long as the students hear it and then use it. It may be a line from a favorite poem, song, adage, proverb, slogan, whatever, as long as it sets up a dominate rhythm and provides the students with a place from which to re-start their language. Of course, the content of the line, as well as the pre-writing discussion of the line, will greatly determine what kind of material will appear in their poems, as the "I Have Seen the Best Minds of My Generation" poems demonstrate.

Other phrases and lines I have used with some good results are:

"When the snow/red leaf falls
I...."

"Walking down the beach
I...."

"Cruising down Broad Street
I...."

"Chillin' on a park bench
I...."

Generally, the length of the line you begin with will determine, approximately, the line-lengths throughout the poem, so short beginning lines will tend to create short-lined poems, and so on. Also, if your first line places the students in a specific, image-laden place, the resultant poems will tend to be imagistic; if, on the other hand, you begin with a more general idea, such as "I have seen the best minds of my generation," you will need to take the additional step, in pre-writing, to ask the students where they see the members of their generation, steering them toward the specific image.

CHAPTER FOURTEEN: MUSIC POEMS

MUSIC POEMS

Music is a wonderful stimulator for writing poetry, but this exercise should be used only after the students have had practice writing poems with images and comparisons. I use the *Music Poem* only after the *Print* and *Place Poems*. This background helps the beginning writers to put themselves in a place which will provide them with images. If they cannot do this, the poems written to music may be too general and abstract.

Students may write *Music Poems* to any kind of music--classical, jazz, rock and roll, tribal chants, church liturgies, the list is endless. The important thing to remember is that the students need some source other than the music for their images and ideas. Following are a few ways to prepare the writers for the Music Poem exercise.

Talk about the "Story" the Music Portrays

One way to prepare for this music exercise is to talk about the themes or stories of the musical piece you are about to play. For instance, if using "The Nutcracker Suite," we talk about the characters and the action of the work, including specific images such as the rats' whiskers and the soldiers marching. I ask the students if they would want to put any of their own characters or images into the work, and if so, which ones? This allows them to start "owning" the piece and to react imaginatively with it.

Then, as they provide images and imaginings, I ask them to make comparisons, too, For instance, the soldiers marching sounds like what? A thousand hearts beating? A thunderous surf? Or, Why are the fairies called Sugar Plum Fairies? What do they look like? And so on. They enjoy this tremendously and are soon calling out more responses than I can put on the board.

Then We Write to the Music

At this point, we play the music and write as we listen. I suggest that everyone writes as long as the music plays, which brings initial moans but, later, pages and pages of good poetry. I also suggest that they listen carefully to the pace of the music, that a slow rhythm might be imaged as the slow drift of snowflakes, and that a fast rhythm might be imaged as a rushing river, or a cavalry charge. Flutes may be doves, drums may be cannons, et cetera. Again, their natural comparison-making abilities usually fill the poems with interesting, poetic associations, as is seen in the following poem, "The Nutcracker Suite," written by a fifth-grade writer, Jenny Hagemeyer:

Poem to Nutcracker Suite

Soldiers marching into battle
like horses running up a mountain,
free and swift
as the battle ends and the last shots
are fired like last rays

133

of the morning sun now coming through
the trees.

Fairies start dancing like dust particles
in the moonlight,
like owls hooting and echoing the song
over and over again.

As I listen, I fall asleep
thinking of myself
floating on water
on a boat built of ice and snow.

A palace of daisies
sweet and soft
comes into view
and horses like mountains
in winter on a map.
I can see the stars of snow
drifting
like pieces of paper.

Peacocks are flying,
spreading their beauty
like a rose opening
as the world rejoices
and deer leap into the air
like airplanes taking off.

I hold out my arms,
they fly and disappear.
Flutes start playing,
melody after melody,
like writing word after word.

Rainbows everywhere,
like a teacher,
a favorite teacher,
writing on a chalkboard.

A flag rises,
red, white, and blue,
I hear the voices of mourning
singing like an old woman
waving her kerchief at her dear son.

I see doves now,
drifting like lost raindrops,
like lost rose petals
falling to the ground.

A man sits next to a woman
looking into her eyes
in a daze,
like they are in space,
all alone.

The snow falls
like the sun rising in the morning.
The ground is covered and far off.

I see two horses
grazing together
like two lonely pencils on my desk.

The rainbows multiplying
like waves on the ocean
sorting out fish and colors.

Now I am flying like the oriole flies,
high above the clouds,
settling on a housetop,
feathers drifting out of nowhere
like a shoemaker
with nails everywhere,
trying to finish before noon.

The rivers rejoice,
overflowing with love and happiness,
like swans floating on a lake
too happy to do anything but rest.

****

Variation: Use Prints to Provide Images for the Music Poem

Another way to help the students to "image" the music is to put prints up around the room and to encourage them to use any of the images which fit the music. As in the *Visuals Poem* exercise, the students should first examine the prints closely, noting any images or imaginings on a sheet of paper. Once they're back in their seats, I'll ask what they saw or imagined in the print, jotting down some of their responses on the board, with, as always, the encouragement to "borrow" whatever they can in order to write. When the images are called out, I encourage comparisons, too, asking what the red boat looks like as it slices through the waves, or what the swirled, hazy gold stars sound like.

After we have plenty of images and imaginings on the board and in our heads, we play some classical music (or jazz, golden oldies, country music, et cetera), usually a work with dramatic tonal shifts that, when they occur, will help the students to shift from one thought or print to another. I ask the students to "write to the music," to try to capture the music's rhythms in their writings, and to use the images and imaginings from the various prints for content. I also write the first line of the poem on the board, "Listening to the music, I remember," and then ask them to write.

Fran Mattfeld, a sixth-grade writer, uses very strong images and comparisons in her poem:

I Remember

Listening to the music
I can remember
running past a windmill in Holland
surrounded by red, blue, yellow tulips,
and sailing in my boat
while watching people stroll
by like gulls soaring in the wind.
I remember watching a vase of roses
while dreaming about a sunny day,
looking out my window
at snow falling
like little white moths
huddling together by a light.
I remember pouring thick
creamy milk
out of a brown pitcher
and into a bowl
for the cat to lap up,
the cat falling asleep
on my lap
as my mother
slowly
closes the cover
of a sad book.

****

This exercise results in poems that "leap," as Robert Bly describes it in his book, *Leaping Poetry,* from one association to another without, necessarily, a logical connection. The poems are often catalogues of "moments" the speaker experiences, with the only connecting thread being the speaker himself. (This is a technique used by Walt Whitman in his great poem, "Song of Myself.") Sarah Russell, a seventh-grade writer, does such leaping in her poem:

Candlelight

Listening to the music I remember...
being at a cemetery
watching the funeral of
Wolfgang
Amadeus
Mozart.
Suddenly
I'm painting
a picture of
a red tree along
a river of fish,
until the music
changes
and I'm sitting
on a chair
with a bouquet
of roses on my lap.
Now I'm sailing
in the blue Chesapeake Bay,
the water looking
like a stone
being shattered
by the bow of the boat
while my father falls
in, the splash like
watching little daggers
of death rising
from the water.
Then it's quiet
and I can hear
the choir of the church,
the sun glimmering
through
the beautiful stained glass
windows,
when I find myself
in Morocco,
surrounded
by beautiful
dark-complexioned women

with
long dark hair
dancing
until the sun comes up
and I open my eyes
to see a single
red rose
in a crystal vase
lit only by
the flickering light
of a candle flame.

****

Not only will this exercise result in very lively associative leaps, it will at the same time help to remedy the straight description or narration that so many beginning poets use in their poems. If your students are writing "story" poems with little imagination, this exercise will probably help them to start breaking those strict narratives and start making greater poetic leaps. Kevin Sinclair, a fifth-grade writer, leaps from image to image in his poem:

The Music and the Tiger

Listening to the music,
  I can remember
lying in my backyard
  smelling roses.

    I can see a baby kitten
       playing with a yellow
           daisy.

And a red cardinal
   on a thin tree branch
 chirping to the sky.

    Now I'm in a stone church
      listening to the chorus
        sing melodies
          to the Lord,
     letting their voices
       go off into space
       like tigers blowing
       fire from their mouths.

****

Michelle Embich, an eighth-grade student, wrote her poem to prints which portrayed women from different countries, but she ends her poem with a fine, introspective moment that moves beyond geographical boundaries:

A Woman

Listening to the music,
I wander through the fields of Holland,
tulips of many colors
shine like crystals in the night.
The windmills spin
and the air about me
is cool and majestic.

In the lonely streets of France,
where no one's around,
ring two silent bells,
clearly in the night.

A woman stands alone,
wishing she were somewhere else.
Somewhere
where no pain can be felt.
Her loneliness fills the room,
her sadness a disease
eating away at her soul.

****

Variation: Use Specific Memories to Provide Images for the Music Poem

Still another way to provide the students with specific sensory details and imaginings while writing to music is by asking them to recall a specific memory (as in the *Memory Poem* exercise), one which has images they can immediately respond to. Before writing, we discuss these memories and I put the recalled images on the board, always trying to get the students to think as concretely as possible, and, again, always encouraging comparisons.

I also mention that music has many "tones," some being sad, some joyful, some, as mentioned previously, fast or slow, and that their poems might try to convey the same tone as the music. For instance, a slow, rolling "drum" rhythm might match with a sad poem, whereas high-pitched violins might recall fiery red cardinals darting in and out of green hedges, and so on. I do not belabor this point, for many of the students will do this "matching" naturally. Once they have plenty of images and imaginings from their memories, we turn on the music and we write.

Farewell

        Listening to the music
I remember the purple church,
    my grandfather lying peacefully
in his glazed oak coffin.
    Taken from never-ending pain
and suffering,
sickness and problems,
    they carry him to his grave
where I place purple roses on top
                and
                    quietly
                        sob.

        --Mark von Oven, seventh grade

        ****

Variation: Write to Oriental Music, Using Han Shan and Other Oriental Images

Another variation of the *Music Poem* which I particularly enjoy is having the students write poems while they listen to Oriental music. (Please see Chapter Twelve, Letter Poem, for more information about writing poems to the Chinese poet, Han Shan.) Since we have already discussed Han Shan's life and have written poems to him, the students have a source of Oriental images upon which to base their poems.

A wonderful tape to play for this exercise is Sam Hamill's *Watching the Waves*, which uses Oriental music as a background for Mr. Hamill's translations of Chinese poems. When using this tape, I strongly encourage the students to use any images or phrases from the poems being read, knowing that, if desired, we may delete these borrowings during revision.

Shannon Sanderson, a fourth-grade writer, created her poem while listening to *Watching the Waves:*

The Music

The music sounds like the Chinese
women hobbling around town
with their red silk kimonos
wrapped tightly around
their legs.

The music sounds like eight
ice skaters playing joyfully
on the ice until the end
of the song,
gentle,

140

as if the best ice skater
came slowly onto the pond
slowly and surely
dancing gallantly
while the townspeople
circle him in amusement.

****

The possibilities of this exercise are truly endless, limited only by the teacher's imagination and energy: war music, love music, church music, nature music, all these types of music, when used with various stories, prints, and/or memories create a vast resource for the writing of poems.

CHAPTER FIFTEEN: PERSONA POEMS

PERSONA POEMS

Most young people like to pretend they are someone or something else, and the Persona Poem exercise encourages this kind of empathy and transferal, what John Keats called "negative capability." Persona poems seem to work best after the students have become comfortable using images, comparisons, and line breaks and, usually, after they have written their Print and Place poems. This background helps to make them comfortable with the use, especially, of images, which in turn will help them to speak better in their new "voice" in the persona poem.

Become Another Person: Using Prints and Stories

To begin, I put prints portraying particular historical or fictional characters such as Zapata, Juliet, John Glenn, or Marie Curie on the board, and, as in the Visuals Poem exercise, I ask the students to examine the prints carefully and to jot down any details that particularly stand out or interest them.

Then I tell a story, true or not, about the characters. For instance, most students enjoy hearing about Zapata's youth, the difficult circumstances he grew up in, the struggles he had throughout his heroic life as a great Mexican revolutionary. I may embellish the story, saying that he was allowed only one glass of milk a day, or that he used to catch rabbits with his bare hands--trying to use details that the students will find interesting and "connect" with, and thus write better poems.

Use Particular Images in the Story

While telling the story about the character, I always use particular images such as the armadillo in the desert or the empty glass of water on the table to prepare the students for their own poems, and I often refer to the images portrayed in the prints, pointing out the yellow cactus flower, the tarantula, et cetera, so the students will see the characters in a physical context/environment. As their images and imaginings are called out, I put them on the board, asking for comparisons that might spark their imaginations: What does the red sun sound like at dawn? What does Zapata's black sombrero look like? What do the desert stars whisper?

After the story is told and the students have many images and imaginings, with comparisons, I ask them to identify with Zapata by asking what they think young Zapata might have heard in the desert at night, what he may have smelled or felt, what words his mother might have said the day he left, and so on. Once they seem to "be" Zapata, I ask them to write and tell us about his life. As the example poems about Zapata and St. Jerome show, this exercise creates some very convincing and interesting poems. (I like to do Zapata and St. Jerome persona poems during the same class period because they both spent a good part of their lives in the desert; students can use some of the Zapata print's desert images in their St. Jerome poem, and vice versa.)

Zapata

I have not long to live,
I die at the break of dawn.

I have fear of dying and I have fear
of hell. I shall stay in my cell
   and pray to the Lord.
It is time for my death but I will
   not go.
I prefer dying in my sleep
   with God upon me.

   --Samuel Rodriguez, fourth grade

     ****

St. Jerome in the Desert

Here I am in this rock-filled land,
watching the old cross with sharp thorns hanging off,
the rocks whispering to each other
like a soft breeze blowing my beard,
a roaring lion at my feet,
and I know God is on my side.
My rock home in the land,
far away and lonely,
I can feel watching me and calling me back,
but I won't go.
I stay on this dirty earth.
I am sorry for my sins.

   --Amy Todd, fifth grade

     ****

Or the students could become a stone Buddha, as Katie Kollet, a fourth-grader, does so well, especially in rendering images of change which mirror Buddha's "reincarnations":

Buddha

I have seen ugly war.
I have seen beautiful birth
like tulips blooming.
I have heard bluebirds
tweeting in the Spring
and snowflakes drifting
to the frozen ground.
I have seen children
going to school
like butterflies

stretching their wings
in the cold air.
After knowing all this
I feel funny being stone,
like an automobile
without an engine.

****

The following poem, written about a deaf character in a print, shows an extremely strong empathy between writer and persona:

Living in a World of Silence

I hear no voices.
I hear no sounds.
I only read
lips and sign language.
I'm defined as handicapped,
but I can cook, dance,
swim, and make figure eights
on the night blue pond.

I may not be able to hear
birds chirping
or frogs croaking --
the wonderful sounds
of spring and summer.
But I can see their
gracious movements --
the many forms of music,
the art of dance.

I may not be able to hear
how you feel,
but I'm a normal person
who smells the deep fragrance
of roses,
the candy-red apples.

I may not hear my children
growing up.
I won't hear their cries.
I won't hear their laughter.
I won't hear their sorrow.
But I'm not blind

to what's going on
in this world!

--Janea Manning, ninth grade

    ****

Variation: Become a Mineral, Plant, Insect, or Animal (or Anything Else)

One variation of the persona poem is to have the students identify with something non-human, be it a mineral, plant, insect, or animal. Again, I provide prints of these things, usually four or five, so the students will have specific images to use in their poems, and we talk about the agate, violet, caterpillar, or muskrat, naming its qualities, its habits, its environment, et cetera. As the images, imaginings, and facts are mentioned, I put them on the board, stressing the more interesting aspects of each, such as, perhaps, that the caterpillar must, at some point of its life, change, or that the violet, such a fragile flower, is often seen growing tenaciously from cracks in walls and sidewalls, and so on.

When the students are enthusiastically pointing out such details, I ask them to become whatever it is they wish to write about, and to tell us what it sees, hears, touches, tastes and smells, as well as imagines and thinks. Since younger people generally have a wonderful capacity for Keats's "negative capability," this exercise often produces some fine poems.

Frog

In the summer
I sit on the lily pads
like floating on icebergs
with nothing around
but the smell
of sweet
cherry blossoms
upon the windblown trees.

The night is cool
and I sing with my friends.
Old Grandfather Toad
the old bag
answers in his gruff voice
like a bear
sharpening his claws
on rough bark.
The young cricket
answers
with his soft
flowing music

echoing through the forest
like dusk
falling upon the earth,
a purple
satin curtain.

Soon the cold day will come
like a blazing fire
in a pine forest
crackling,
like the uneven beat
of horses' hooves
upon the paved road
and it will all be gone.

    --Jenny Hagemeyer, fourth grade

       ****

Variation: Become a Fictional Character

Another variation of this exercise is good to use after the students have read a work that contains a character or characters with which they may be able to identify. For instance, if the class has been reading *MacBeth* or *Romeo and Juliet*, ask them to become one of the characters and to write a poem from that perspective. Of course, the identification can only take place once the students know the character(s), so they will have the sensory and imaginative details to draw on once they begin to write.

Although I have used this device often, the best poem of its type came from a young writer who was in one of my former student's classes. Pam Johnson, a teacher in the Pittsburgh school district, assigned a persona poem after teaching *Romeo and Juliet*; the following is one of the results.

The Honeymoon Is Over

    The prince has let Romeo come back!
        What am I to do?
    The excitement just no longer exists.
        Let's face it,
The spice is gone from our unseasoned relationship.
      Oh, impassive feelings,
        Enchanted boredom,
    What makest me love thee no longer?
        Spiteful Cupid has taken his arrow back!
        Like a glass of flat champagne,
           The thrill is gone!

--Michelle Watson, tenth grade

****

Or, from the same class, another persona poem:

Paris' Thoughts

> Thinking about her
> She being such an innocent beast
> A Lovely Sight to All

Wondering why she betrayed me
Wondering why she loved Romeo, the immortal plague
Wondering how I could rescue her from such

> A Piteous Piteous Predicament

Thinking of the way it could be
Wishing for the way it should be
Thinking of my sweet Juliet
> As I lower my head.

--Carla Bailey, tentn grade

****

Note: It is important that, in preparing to write, the students discuss the characters in specific sensory details and phrases; this will anchor their poems in the world of the persona and thus prevent it from floating away in abstractions.

After I use the persona poem exercise in various schools, teachers often write to tell me they have used it in history (become Hitler), science (become an ant), literature (become Hemingway's "old man" or the sharks!) with great success, for the students will not only learn the facts about their subject, they will also use those facts in a personally meaningful and enjoyable creation of their own--the persona poem.

CHAPTER SIXTEEN: MEMORY POEMS

MEMORY POEM

This is a very effective exercise to use after the students have written Visuals, Place, and Quiet Poems, all of which will help the writers to use concrete, unique sensory perceptions in their poems.

I ask the students to recall one of their most powerful, lasting memories and, as they are recalling it, to write down any sensory images that come to mind. Tell them these images do not have to belong literally to the experience, and, in fact, many should be imaginary, for the mind has a way of connecting details we would not ordinarily combine. I encourage them to use the names of streets, of cities, of old neighbors, a grandfather's favorite flower, an uncle's favorite dog. These names have a power of their own, I stress, and can conjure up new and fresh insights as well as additional sensory details -- all of which will help them to continue writing.

It is also important that they note the unique characteristics of the remembered person or moment, that they capture the physical details peculiar to each. For example, I tell the students that I continually associate the image of an imitation pearl necklace with the memory of my mother. Or I mention my father's Golden Eagle bread truck which idled in the falling snow of Cohoes, New York on winter mornings.

Once they understand the significance of such remembered images and have jotted some of them down, we practice making comparisons. For example, what does the remembered blue ice on the gutter sound like, or what does the remembered glass of milk look like? When the comparisons are being said regularly, they are almost ready to write.

At this point, I like to read them a few memory poems written by other students, again encouraging them to use any image or idea that might inspire their own writing. Lisa Mendock, a fifth-grade writer, shows an adult understanding in her poem:

Remember

        Standing by the river,
I remember my Grandpa milking
        the cows on the farm
            in the dusk of the day.
        Meanwhile, in the house,
Grandma cooked Sunday supper, with
        the crispy brown turkey sizzling
            in the oven
and little ones playing in the hay.

Now there are only the trees and the leaves
        of golden color,
and the waving lilies of the field,
        while
everyone gathers around the brown living room

laughing about the old times.

****

Older students often do quite well with the Memory Poem, also, as the following high school student poems show:

Jonathan's Grave

Staring at the cold gray stone,
the rain falls around me.
Mist seems to rise,
meeting the dark gray sky.
Voices call inside my head,
drawing me nearer
to a time and a place,
building castles in sand.
Waves wash in and destroy the laughter.
Cold wind chills me to the bone,
a warm hand touched my shoulder.
I turn to see who wanted me,
but all I see is the cold gray stone.

   --Stephanie Fisher, tenth grade

   ****

Them

Grandfather w/ one arm & no teeth
  that's him putting 3 heaping
  spoons of sugar in his coffee.

Highhairsprayed hair tight small
skirts eyes closed to the future.

Laughing crowds.

Sneaking through
    her precious flowers
I can't get my teeth out.

Combing my Nana's
hair and the smell of it and
how thin it was.

--Ann Barth, twelfth grade

****

Yellow Amaryllis

Playing hide and seek
in Grammy Steigerwalt's yard
hovering behind the dilapidated corncrib
listening for tacit footsteps
creeping up on me in the knowing grass
they draw near, searching me out

Gram calls that dinner is ready
later, playing in the old wooden toy chest
blocks and empty thread spools
that once held gallant strands of the rainbow

Gram adorned in an old gingham apron
and a flowered cotton dress
resting in the rocking chair
in the kitchen corner
darning socks and patching holes
saying how chilly it is
pulling the thin gray sweater
over her thin shoulders

We go out to weed the flowerbeds
for the last time before winter attacks
fall is the time to plant bulbs
my favorites were the ones called Amaryllis
the pictures were intrinsic
but their color was not mentioned

The service held at Nestor's
I felt obligated to attend
that cold December day
careful not to meet
her blank, staring eyes
Time crept up
spring arrived in glory
yellow Amaryllis blooming
brilliant in that yard again.

--Terri Faust, tenth grade

****

Note: I think it is particularly important, especially for a memory poem, that the students do not determine beforehand what outcome their poems will have; that is, they may know they want to write about an afternoon on the beach with their mothers, but they shouldn't decide, before they begin, whether it should be a "happy" or "sad" poem. The images of the memory should carry the writers, hopefully, into new, unexplored territory, so that an experience they thought was sad may turn out to be happy in the poem, and vice versa. If the writers are willing to be carried by the poem, they will end up in places they didn't expect, and that is one of the joys of writing.

PRAISE POEMS (ODES)

Students of all ages love to praise things, from the grain of sand to the whirling planets and stars, so the poem of praise, the ode, is a writing exercise they naturally enjoy creating.

Before attempting the ode, however, the students should be familiar with Image making (Chapter One), Rhythm (Chapter Two), Comparison making (Chapter Three) and, finally, Word Music (Chapter Four). Once these basic elements of poetry writing are covered, the only job left to the teacher is to prepare the students, through discussion and presentation of models, on how to begin.

For instance, if the odes were to be about fruit, various kinds of fruit could be brought to class and passed around so the students could feel, smell, see, and yes, even listen and taste them! Perhaps drawings or paintings of fruits could be posted, the students encouraged to refer to the artist and painting. Or a vocabulary of exotic fruits might be passed out, listing detailed information about each fruit, including country of origin, number of seeds, et cetera. The more intellectual and sensual information the students have, the better the prospects for their poems will be.

Then, to show the students that they may write an ode to *anything*, not just a "poetical subject," such as a rose, I read them a couple of Pablo Neruda's odes. (Sections of a few of Neruda's poems are presented here, so the teacher may get a sense of image, rhythm, and overall tone in such poems. For more examples, please see SELECTED ODES OF PABLO NERUDA, translated by Margaret Sayers Peden. Los Angeles: University of California Press1990.)

Ode to My Socks

Maru Mori brought me
a pair
of socks
knitted with her own
shepherd's hands,
two socks soft
as rabbits.
I slipped
my feet into them
as if
into
jewel cases
woven
with threads of
dusk
and sheep's wool.

Audacious socks,
my feet became

two woolen
fish,
two long sharks
of lapis blue
shot
with a golden thread,
two mammoth blackbirds,
two cannons,…

Or, on a sadder note, Neruda's "Ode to a Saffron Finch":

I buried you in the garden:
a grave
no larger
than my open hand,
earth,
the cold
earth of the south
slowly covering
your feathers,
the yellow sunbeams,
the black lightning flashes
of your snuffed out body…
Oh, innocent
bird,
I knew you living,
electric,
vital,
melodious,
your body was
a fragrant
arrow,
you hopped
along my arms and shoulders,
independent, untamed,
black of black stone
and pollen yellow….

Or, finally, "Ode to a Stamp Album"

Butterflies,
ships,
sea shapes, corollas,
leaning towers,
dark eyes, moist and
round as grapes,

album smooth
as
a
slippery
fish,
with thousands
of glistening
scales,
each page
a
racing
charger
in search of
distant pleasures, forgotten
flowers!...

As the teachers and students soon realize, Neruda considers the entire world, and beyond!) as potential material for his odes, as should the beginning writers. So, after reading a couple of his odes, I ask the students what they might write about, getting such responses as nail polish, writer's block, and even road kill! At this point, we write, creating poems such as the few examples presented here.

Ode to Nail Polish

Perfect glassine bottles
Full of the colors of the sun
    Or the earth
    Or the moon
Depending on the feeling

    Cover fingernails
With metallic luster
    Hide them
    Hide me
From the world

Black and purple
By far my favorite two
    Some orange
    Some Silver
Cover these nails

    Keep them under
    Away from people
    From sadness
    From loneliness

Dead nails on my fingertips

Jason Byrd, ninth grade

The student who wrote the next poem said she could not think of anything to write about, so she wrote about that:

Ode to Writer's Block

You are the block that keeps my hand still.
  I sit here in boredom thinking
You are the bolt and nut that tightens my head,
  causing me to pound it in pain.
You are the eraser marks decorating my paper,
  scouring its welcoming face.
You surround my mind, darkening my days,
  blackening my white.
You are my handicap holding back
  my creative touch.
I despise your arrival, yet once you're here
  I tell your story and you disappear.

Jennifer Rowe, tenth grade

Carolyn Kerchof, a sixth grader, praises and empathizes with a bug squashed on her windshield.

Ode to the Bug on My Windshield

Oh buggy, how I pity you!
    Holding on to life,
While the wind whips you about.
        Dancing
      A deadly waltz,
    Alone, without a partner.
Why do you make me feel so sad?
      Lost in the world.
      On my windshield.
    Do you remind me of me?
    About to be blown away
      by the forces of life.

Or, on another, equally humorous note:

Ode to My Shoelaces

Old and wrinkly, tangled and worn,

shoelaces with the flat woven sides.
You are the ice in my water,
the fizz in my Coke.
Without you, my multicolored sneakers
    are nothing more than shoes.
Mangled and tattered, but always tied,
my shoelaces with the broken plastic tips
pull and tighten around my feet,
loop in two neat intricate bows.
Heaven help me when you come untied!
I loop you, I swoop you,
shoelaces, I love you!

Elsa Buss, seventh grade

And, with a darker humor, tenth-grader Duston Steel's poem:

Ode to Road Kill

You're like the furry cream added to the roadside coffee.
You're like a living raspberry donut that had its filling oozed out,
the energizer bunny that finally stopped going,
the flattened feathery collage of bird-like stupidity,
a symbol to all creatures of why the chicken did not cross the road,
a testimony to all felines of how curiosity killed the cat.
You possess the ability to ruin a new pair of shoes and turn
    the strongest stomach.
You represent the battle of creatures and cars.
You're a dwelling for many homeless parasite families,
the speed bump needed to slow down the speeding driver.
Oh road kill, what would we do without you!

And, finally, Carol Gaertner, a seventh grader, who writes about not being able to write.

Ode to My Pencil AKA Writer's Block

Sharp, silvery-gray graphite tip,
Strong cylinder of yellow wood,
        Extra-hard #4
    With a worn lime eraser
        Stubbornly refusing
To create images out of words.

CHAPTER SEVENTEEN: HOLOCAUST POEMS

HOLOCAUST POEMS

Many schools have sections of their curriculum dedicated to learning about the Holocaust, and thus teachers are continually looking for ways the students may express their new-gained knowledge. Because the Holocaust contains such strongly emotional material, the genre of poetry, which has been the vehicle for expressing strong emotion throughout the ages, is a most appropriate and powerful form for the students' expressions.

Relying on the principles discussed in earlier chapters of this book, the teacher/writer may prepare the students for their writing by providing a good supply of images (posters, slides, visits to museums, et cetera (as discussed in Chapter One, Images), a rhythmical form (breath span, as discussed in Chapter Two, Line Breaks), and a way to begin (a set-up, as discussed in Chapter Five, How to Begin).

To begin, we brainstorm their images and ideas about the Holocaust, and I write their responses on the board, always urging them to be as specific and concrete as possible; so "mass slaughter" becomes a "mound of corpses" and "constant persecution" becomes a "number branded on wrist skin," and so on. Those students who have learned about the Holocaust, whether from a field trip to the Holocaust Museum, class lectures, or other experiences, will have a strong core for such brainstorming; the more they know before we write, the better.

At this point, I put up posters or show slides of the Holocaust, emphasizing the images presented, such as the yellow star, the sifting ashes, the piles of shoes left behind, until the students can "put themselves there" poetically, using what Keats calls Negative Capability, the ability to identify with the poetic experience.

The next step is to help them to make striking comparisons, so I will ask what the yellow star *sounds* like, forcing them to stretch their imaginations. Or what time sounds like when one is a prisoner in the camps. This kind of warm-up helps them to use similes and metaphors in their poems, and thus breaks up the strict narrative that can often make their writing seem more like stories than poems.

Once the students are calling out their images, referring to their own knowledge as well as the visual aids, and making imaginative comparisons, I set them up for the writing exercise with a reference to the Chekhov story about a carriage driver who is waiting for his rich client to leave his party and be driven home. I tell them how the driver stands alone in the bitter Russian winter night, talking to his horse about the death of his wife and children the previous week from the plague. This man had no one else in the world to talk to about his grief, I emphasize, and then ask them to imagine they are there, feeling the cold, the darkness, the grief. Once they are empathizing to the point where they say such things as "My hands are blue," or "My words turn to icicles," or "The horse's breath is the only warmth in the night," then I ask them to imagine they have survived the Holocaust, as this driver has survived the plague, and they can tell their tales of horror to no one but the horse. I ask them to put themselves there, in that freezing Russian night, beside the horse, and to talk to it. The following poems, or sections of poems, are a few results of this exercise.

Talking into the Horse's Ear

Talking into the horse's ear
I tell it about the sound of shovels
digging ditches of death
the unsuspecting diggers will lie in,
and of how time completely stopped
when I shared a bunk with a corpse,
the clank of pipes carrying, no doubt,
gas to the cold showers.
I whisper into its ear about the music
that raced my heart and thoughts
as I waited for water or gas
to pour from the nozzles.
I could feel the horse sadden
as I told him of the rhythmic clicking
made by the Nazi's boots coming
to take me, and the clank
of the train taking thousands,
millions, to their deaths….

Aaron Wynkop, seventh grade

Talking into the Horse's Ear

While I wait in the cold depths of night,
I whisper into the horse's ear,
tell it of the yellow star
like millions and millions
of people in gas chambers
gasping for their last breath of air.
I tell it about the crematories
waiting to play their song of death,
how time stopped when they beat my father
with a bone-tipped whip, slashing him with blood
in the sooty grass. I tell it about my mother's
comforting voice when I heard it the last time,
how it melted into my brain,
and the horse turns its head away in disgust,
chills running down our backs.

Grant Gavran, eighth grade

World War II Memories

Talking to the horse

I tell it how the yellow star
   sounds like the wailing of bodies
   and the hiss of escaping gas,
about my mother's gold locket
   hanging around a German's neck.
   I tell it about the Jews, packed
    by thousands into the death trains
knowing they would never see their homeland again.
I tell it about the bottomless pits of bodies,
   only their memories remaining.
I tell the horse that time sounds
   like my mother's last breath…
and I weep as the horse moves its head,
   offering me a place to cry on,
    the cold of the night
    all too familiar
    as I return from the bleak past
    to the equally harsh present
    filled with everlasting snow.

Christopher Cwynar, eighth grade

Bobbie Decker, an eighth grade student, uses strong metaphors and personification in her poem about the Holocaust:

Images of Despair

Whispering into the horse's ear, I tell it
about the curdling screams of the innocent
ripping through my skin,
fear embedded in the air,
the stench of the Nazis.

Whispering into the horse's ear, I tell it
about opening my nostrils to the full reality,
the blanket of silence
suffocating all,
the whip of violence,
slicing.

Whispering into the horse's ear, I tell it
about the skeleton hanging silently
from the rope of despair,
carried away with the icy breath
of hate and oppression,
vapor steaming from the mouth

full of illness,
waiting to digest our hopes.

Or, finally, a Holocaust poem written while music was played in the classroom:

The Holocaust

>As the violin screeches
>>I tell the horse
>of the yellow star that sounds like
>>a Jewish man
>>hit by a bullet
>fired from the SS officer's gun.
>>As the clarinet plays
>I tell the horse about my father's ring
>>melting, just one more valuable gone.
>>As the oboe plays low notes
>>I tell the horse
>about time that sounds like the cries
>of emaciated bodies going up in flames.
>>As the silence rolls on
>>I tell the horse…
>of Jews tossed into mountains of dead bodies,
>and of skeletons in crematories
>>and of ashes….

Devang Amin, eighth grade

CHAPTER EIGHTEEN: NATURE POEMS—

NEW AND SELECTED APPROACHES

TO WRITING ABOUT NATURE

NATURE POEMS: NEW AND SELECTED APPROACHES TO WRITING POEMS ABOUT NATURE

Student writers or all ages love to write about nature; from kindergarten to graduate school to nursing homes, writers hear the call of nature and the words flow. Our task, as teachers of poetry writing, is to help these writers depict their views of nature in original and powerful ways. The following approaches may help them accomplish this: 1. accurate, specific observation; 2. extension of images in unusual, unexpected ways, including the use of comparisons; and 3. several prompts that will help guide the "nature" poems down excitingly unique paths.

Unique images will help create strong nature poetry. To show these beginning writers that established poets do indeed rely strongly on the image, I hand out copies of William Carlos Williams' short poem, "Sparrows among Dry Leaves" and a section of his longer poem, "The Sparrow." Before reading the poems aloud, though, I ask them to note especially the specific images Dr. Williams uses, and to see if they can find anything in the poetry that surprises them. Then we read:

Sparrows among Dry Leaves

The sparrows by the iron fence post--
hardly seen for the dry leaves
that half cover them--
stirring up the leaves, fight
and chirp stridently, search and
peck the sharp gravel to
good digestion....

And here are several lines from Dr. Williams' longer poem, "The Sparrow":

Once
    at El Paso
            toward evening,
I saw--and heard!--
    ten thousand sparrows
            who had come in from
the desert
        to roost. They filled the trees
            of a small park. Men fled
(with ears ringing!)
        from their droppings,
                leaving the premises
to the alligators
        who inhabit
                the fountain....

The students greatly enjoy both of these works and are quick to point out the specific images of "iron fence post," "dry leaves," "sharp gravel," "ten thousand sparrows," and "alligators" in the "fountain." They are also very alert to the unexpected actions that occur in the poems, such as the dry leaves half covering the sparrows, the fact that they "fight/and chirp stridently" and, of course, in the excerpt from "The Sparrow," how the men flee from the ten thousand sparrows' "droppings." From this discussion, we come to the conclusion that a good poet won't just have a sparrow in a tree --for that would be far too boring. Instead, the poet will strive to make the sparrow stand out somehow, which leads us to our next step.

CONTRASTING COLORS AND TEXTURES HELP THE NATURAL IMAGE STAND OUT

At this point we discuss how the "hard" images such as "iron fence post," "sharp gravel," "alligators" and "fountain" contrast with the softness of the sparrows and thus make the sparrows stand out more--the reader sees them more clearly because of the contrasting images. Then I mention that Dr. Williams also wrote a poem about a cardinal perched on a snow-covered evergreen hedge, asking them why they think he did that. Again, they're quick to note the contrasting colors, the white snow and green hedge making the cardinal's redness even more vivid. Jennifer Ring, an eighth grader, emphasizes such contrasting colors in her poem, "My Yellow Cockatiel":

My Yellow Cockatiel

My yellow cockatiel
by the blue wall
sits on its perch
chirping away,
waking us up
to the morning shade
with loud, cheerful song.
That's my yellow cockatiel
by the blue wall.

Jim Addlespurger, a teacher in the Pittsburgh School District, also uses color contrasts in his poem, "Cardinal."

Cardinal

Wing flapping
on the wet windshield
waiting
to be one with the ground.

Flight in the neon-blue
car in the night,
eighty miles an hour

170

wipers whip
cardinal to the cold ground.

Red stains
through drops of rain
like teardrops in a driver's eye.

I also mention that Allen Ginsberg's fine poems, "Sunflower Sutra" and "In Back of the Real," are about sunflowers in unusual places. Then I ask them where they think, given the principle of contrast we've already discussed, Ginsberg placed his sunflowers. I'll sometimes give them a hint, saying that the poet's setting is not a field or a garden (again, too boring!) but is man-made. They enjoy this game and are soon placing the sunflower beside a green dumpster or black Volvo. It comes as no surprise to them when I say Ginsberg placed his sunflowers, bedraggled as they are, beside locomotives, a tank factory and an asphalt highway. (These poems may be found in Allen Ginsberg's book of poetry, *Howl*, published by City Lights Books, 1956.)

At this point, I'll read the beginning of "Sunflower Sutra," "I walked on the banks of the tincan banana dock and sat down under the huge shade of a Southern Pacific locomotive,..." reminding the students that the poet places the sunflower in this unusual setting for dramatic contrast, and that he ends the poem praising the grimy sunflower as "A perfect beauty of a sunflower!" I'll also read "In Back of the Real," emphasizing such lines as "A flower lay on the hay on the asphalt highway,..." for the dramatic contrast between the natural sunflower and the man-made locomotive and asphalt.

(Here are a few stanzas from "Sunflower Sutra," to show Ginsberg's dramatic contrasts at work"

...and the gray Sunflower poised against the sunset, crackly bleak and dusty with the smut and
    and smog and smoke of olden locomotives in its eye—

corolla of bleary spikes pushed down and broken like a battered crown, seeds fallen out of its
face,
    soon-to-be-toothless mouth of sunny air, sunrays obliterated on its hairy head like a dried wire
    spiderweb,

leaves stuck out like arms out of the stem, gestures from the sawdust root, broke pieces of plaster
    fallen out of the black twigs, a dead fly in its ear,

Unholy battered old thing you were, my sunflower, O my soul, I loved you then!)

We usually practice this method of contrasting images for ten minutes or so, until the students feel comfortable placing yellow roses beside green garbage cans, or bluejays beside red Honda Civics. Then they are ready to write their nature poems in unique ways, as is demonstrated in the following poems.

Ugly Pigeons

A flock of ugly pigeons
landed downtown
on an old, brown
bench to eat bread crumbs.

I glanced from the ice
cream shop and raced
out the door, my gait
taking the birds

by surprise. I
saw them jetting by
the blazing hot sun,
melting over top of us.

I held up my hand.
I waved goodbye.

Laura Zlatos, seventh grade

Lucy Ware, an associate director of the Western Pennsylvania Writing Project, used the contrast method in her poem, "City Park," creating a "soiled pamper" image to counter the softer, "nature" images.

City Park

Plum, warm from the trunk,
eaten quick,
as juice pools
held by tart purple skin
while the robin pecks
at a soiled pamper
under the park bench
and periwinkle pushes
against shining slate.

Krystal Robinson, a seventh grader, also balances her nature images with the harder, man-made "black car" image:

Suspiciously

   Bluejay
fluttering beside the black car,
  looking around suspiciously.

   Chirp, Chirp, Chirp, Chirp,

Fiddle De Flaw

There came his mate, flapping
    her wings,
soaring through the pink roses,
   the light blue sky.

Or, more simply, this poem by David Emerick, a fifth grader:

Red Rose

blooming in a subway

      beside careless passengers

  while the train engine blasts.

And, finally, this poem by Shane Pearce, a third grader:

Yellow Rose
    blooming
  in a purple
      turtle
        shell
while
  a bluejay
     perches
on an old   broken   down   red
    Volvo.

COMPARISONS TO ENLIVEN NATURE'S IMAGES

Before turning to full-blown writing prompts, I like to stir the students' imaginations with some comparison making, that attribute of the poet which Aristotle claimed to be the most important. Again, my intention in this exercise is to help the student writers to see natural images in fresh, exciting ways, knowing that such a perspective also will overflow into their later poems.

The "twist" I like to put on this exercise is to ask what a (any color) rose *sounds* like. If I ask them to use any of their other senses in the comparison making, such as what a blue rose *looks* like, their responses tend to be too realistic, less imaginative. I stress that their rose can sound like anything they want, the only limit is their imagination. This exercise may result in work ranging from a one line comparison to a thirty line poem, depending on the writer's interest and energy. Here are some examples.

Yellow Rose

The yellow rose
sounds like
the gentle buzz of
honey bees collecting
nectar next to
an old, beat-up, blue
Mercedes Benz.

Michael Stuck, fifth grade

Aunt Anna

A yellow rose sounds like
damp leaves on the cracked sidewalk
in October
when the wind turns clean,
shaking sweet apples
on backyard branches
as Aunt Anna smokes
her grief into amber
glasses of Jim Beam.

Connie Weiss, high school teacher

Dinging

Yellow rose sounds
   like dripping water
   from the backyard spigot
   dinging an old tin bucket.

Megan Pfenninger, seventh grade

The following student, Erin Dolan, a fourth grader, liked comparisons so much he used them throughout his poem, in much the same way as Pablo Neruda, the great Chilean poet, does, to keep adding images of his world into the work.

My Periwinkle Rose

My periwinkle rose sounds
like: my grandfather's pipe
   and has
the sweet scent of his tobacco.
The vibrance of its opening
   is deafening

like a match loudly glimmering
in the eerie glow
of a child's moon
as a cardinal signals
its bugle-like call,
an awakening.
Like: fresh dew
of a morning's
crispness.
Like: a floral dress
on a woman thinking about her life,
when she was a child
dancing in the square,
where she carried a basket,
her own,
filled
with the eggs
of her orange chicken.
Now, like: a trickling
of a fountain
seeming to answer
the cardinal's call,
the purple waters
flowing off the sides
and the scents
of the mint-fresh water,
all
entrancing me
and I react to the agony
of the dying flower,
the one,
musical
and peacefully
dying periwinkle rose.

Jo Dzombak, now a retired middle school teacher, wrote a rose poem during a session with her seventh graders:

Roses

I swore I'd always
love the soft whispers
of the patrician pink rose
best,
but then
the teasing flamenco guitar

of the peach-tipped coral
sounded.

And Mary Savanick, also a middle school teacher, melded the image of a newborn into her rose poem.

Rose Sounds

The red rose sounds like
   the newborn screaming
and shrill in the lonely night.
   The milky white
vase stands staunch with weight,
   Baby's Breath and fern
hold roses steady
   under gusts from March winds.

EXTENDING THE COMPARISON POEM ABOUT NATURE WITH WORDS SUCH AS "WHILE," "NOW," AND "SUDDENLY"

Poems written to the above exercise (or, for that matter, practically any poem) may be extended, especially if the student writers, once they've run out of words with their initial comparison, write a word such as "while," "now," or "suddenly" and then continue their poem with another image that is not connected (supposedly!) with the first image. This technique will also help the students to break their usual narrative impulse and create more associational jumps, what Robert Bly calls "Leaping Poetry." Here are some results.

Red Rose

The red rose sounds like
   blood
  on white snow
   in winter,
the blood making its own
   small river
in the snowy creek bed
   while
a bluejay screams like
   a town crier
    sensing
   the red river,
and the children can only
   stand and stare
   in wonder.

Amy Griffin, fifth grade

176

Jean Brown, a high school teacher, uses "while" to extend her poem that also uses the contrasts between nature and man-made images discussed above.

Middle Age

Sitting in the car at night, she can hear
  crickets
      singing to their mates,
      tiny buzz saws rubbing legs
like the voices of old boyfriends
  on late summer nights.
While fireflies turn on, turn off,
  she feels
      the car seat's taut canvas cloth
      on the back of her thighs
      and smells stale beer.
The red dash light reflects
  from the white underside of a maple leaf
  while Dylan chants, squawks, fades,
      playing "Blowin' in the Wind."

Marc Ripper, a fourth grader, uses two extension words to bring him to his surprising, delightful poem end:

The Blue Rose

  A blue rose sounds like dust
falling fast in the living room air
    while, far out in the Atlantic,
     fish jump up to clouds
and the sun
    beats down
on the cold breezy beach where,

  suddenly,

I feel like an angel
  dancing on a grain of sand.

USING OTHER COMPARATIVE TERMS TO WRITE NATURE POETRY: RED LEAF, SNOW, TIME, ET CETERA

Other possible comparative terms that will infuse the students' writing about nature with unique perspectives and phrasings are "What does a red leaf sound like?" and "What does the snow sound like?" (There are numerous other comparative terms that might be used here, such as diamond, star or green moon—whatever the teacher thinks would "fire" the students' imaginations.)

Red Leaves

Red leaves
        fall
  in autumn,
sounding like an ant's
    crying
        as he drops
    from the fragile
petal of a violet,
    then silence
in which I suddenly hear
        my father
            sleeping
    as the coffee
      drips
    from the silver pot.

Julie Kaufman, sixth grade

Jim Addlespurger, the Pittsburgh high school teacher cited for his poem "Cardinal" in the contrast section above, wrote a full two-page poem about the sounds a red leaf makes when it falls. Following are a few stanzas:

When the Red Leaf Falls

When the red leaf falls,
it echoes with pounding relief,
it sets itself free
from the barren tree....

When the red leaf falls,
the canyons cry
out their echoing, joyful
call from wall to wall

and the yellow wheat
in the valley below
blows a sigh of relief--
grief is blown from the exhaust
of every downtown truck
delivering pain and happiness
in choking stutters and stops.

When the red leaf falls,
the walls of China crumble,
the ocean roars
and spits and spins
the howling winds,
like some pumped up balloon
that hasn't been tired,
being set free beneath
the blue-black sky,
speckled with fluff
of cotton candy clouds
from Montana to Madrid,
covering the continents with
blankets of blaring red
and gold passion....

Tricia Buckman, a fifth grader, compares snow in her poem, capturing its quietness through her image selection.

Snow

Snow sounds like
a white horse in a field of daisies,
an old man's white beard,
a cloud in the sky,
a white sheet under a Christmas tree
in a room with no furniture,
just blank walls.

Or the students may compare a term which is not usually thought of as natural with terms from nature, as is illustrated in the following examples.

Time

Time sounds like
a flow of geese
flying across the blue sky
in the noon of the day
with the wind blowing
across the whole earth.

Donna Bellesfield, fourth grade

Fireworks

Fireworks are like
tiny rainbows of fire
bursting and flaring--
they can make
a simple boom
or a complex flower
in the night.

Tom Anfuso, fifth grade

PROMPTS TO MOTIVATE ORIGINAL, UNIQUE POEMS ABOUT NATURE

When the students understand and enjoy writing about natural images that are original and exciting, and when they know how to make those images stand out and extend, we turn to writing prompts that will motivate longer, more involved poems. However, each prompt must also have its own "twist," some element that will help the student writers create fresh, surprising poems which can reinvigorate and transform the usual cliches of nature writing such as red sun sets and blooming red roses. These twists are essential and, if the students have done well so far, they will have no trouble at all in following these new directives.

"LISTENING CAREFULLY" IN NATURE POEMS

One of my favorite nature writing exercises is to have the students listen to the sounds they might hear in nature--always stressing that the sounds do not have to be real, they can be (and often should be) imagined. To prepare them for writing, I'll ask the students to list some specific images from a very quiet time they experienced in nature, a time which may have occurred in a field, the woods, or on a lake, and so on. I ask them to think specifically of things they might hear, such as twigs snapping, a chorus of bullfrogs, or a catfish leaping. I write their images on the board as they say them, reminding the class that anyone can "borrow" any of these images to keep writing if they run out of imagination.

Once the board is full I ask them what they now can hear with what I call their inner ear (the ear of their imagination) in this special place of nature, encouraging them to hear such things as ants singing as they march up the oak tree's bark, or their grandfather's breath sighing in the blue spruce needles. This, I remind them, is the realm of the imagination, and their nature poems should contain both the real and the imagined. I also remind them to use comparisons, as they have in their earlier exercises. Now, when they are ready to write, I add that they should be able to write a full page of poetry during the class period—a goal they usually attain. Then we write.

The Willow

In the woods
as silent as a fly,
I heard a willow
as it grew and grew,
its lovely arms

looking more and more
like tentacles
turning orange
in the setting sun.
Listening carefully
I heard
the field mice
walking, climbing
wheat stalks thin
as thread. Soon,
they said,
the willow will
come alive
and dance
soft as a cloud
in any wind.

Melissa Tavares, fourth grade

Or, with more ominous intimations, a sixth grader, Zachary Harris, writes:

On the Lake

Sitting here
In the steel gray canoe.
Summer. Dusk.
I hear crickets chirping
In the tall grass on shore.
I hear the gentle dip
Of the canoe paddle into
The deep green surface
Of the lake. Now
My father's voice
In the canoe. With me.
Comforting. Time
Stands still
As though frozen on the lake,
Although storms brew
Behind the lonely hills
On the dark horizon.
I feel them.
I hear their shadows
Creeping over the lake.

These "Listening Carefully" in nature poems work well with older students, too, as the two following works by teachers demonstrate.

Quiet by Berries

An abandoned railroad bridge
near still, tall grass.
The motionless water
reflecting my feet
dangling, dirty and bare,
silence here.

A distant screen door slams,
a truck stirs dust, grumbling
upon the over-burdened road,
disturbs crows from hiding.

Hot sun, sizzling my shoulders.
Soothing scent of berries
ripened among thorn bushes
that ripped naked skin,
left scratches
while memory sounds
drift across rustling leaves.

Tami Jo Turchich

Bob Werner, teacher who also farms, put his own slant on his quiet nature poem:

Harvest Time

Others now sat at the springhouse trough
    and water splashed their denim legs.
I stood up, passed marbled shoes
And left the cool behind, hearing
Steps past the locust I had split,
Apple, oak and pine.
Blow-flies hummed the barn floor chaff,
Sam's granary tan and full.
I scooped my hands
To cotton, blue-cuffed sleeves,
Listened to falls of wheat
Sift my fingers and palms.
The dust sighed by and
Then I dipped again.
A clover mow rattled pungent
    against the unpegged door,
The window tacked aside.

Across the ridge, I saw my home
Ablaze in August light.
There, with bins of dry threshed grain,
I stood cradled safe.

And, as a lighter, final example, "Sailing," by Renee DeHart, a fourth grader:

Sailing

Sailing in my light
blue sailboat,
I hear the white waves
prancing and dancing
while the stars sing
a short, beautiful lullaby
where I lie,
my eyes deep in thought.
The moonlight sprays
on the silent
sandy beach,
the sails whisper
like a blanket swaying
on a gentle breeze,
as my shoelaces dance
in a lovely rhythm
up and down my feet.

With older students, I will mention that beginning a poem with a reference to a particular place, which I call "grounding the poem," is a process seen in many poems written by such fine poets as James Wright, Gary Snyder, D.H. Laurence, Elizabeth Bishop and so on.

One Variation on "Listening in Nature" Poem: "The Quietest Moment of My Life"

A variation on the "Listening in Nature" poem is to give the students the first line, "The quietest moment of my life," and to have them write from it, once again emphasizing what they can hear, both real and imagined, in their special places in nature. Here are a few illustrative results.

Dad

The quietest moment
of my life
was when me
and my Dad
went fishing,
it sounded
like rain drops

splashing
into the water
and
fish jumping
and
the reel like crickets
as the water
kept running
downstream.

Douglas Grietzes, fifth grade

Quiet

The quietest moment of my life
is just before I drop to sleep
and I hear the snap of sparks
in the downstairs fireplace.
I hear the bullfrog croaking in the lake,
and the crackling caterpillars
munching heartily on leaves
until they are all gone.
I hear the chirps of crickets
like fiddlers in the night...
all is quiet as a leaf
drifting to the ground,
quiet.

Jeff Krouse, sixth grade

Lastly, Jennifer Hager, a fifth grader, captures an Emersonian transcendental union of speaker with nature in her poem "The Quietest Moment of Snow":

The Quietest Moment of Snow

is a bright and sunny
Saturday morning in January
after a heavy snowfall
with crystal white snow
covering the ground
and hiding the cars in driveways
and along the streets.
No one is moving,
everything is still

as I look out my bedroom window
down at the glistening snow.

A Second Variation on the "Listening in Nature" Poem: the "Spider in the Garden" Poem

This exercise works particularly well with students from K-sixth grades, for they have few, if any, inhibitions about "becoming" a spider and "hearing" things as they crawl around the garden. As in earlier exercises, we first gather our specific images from the garden, be they plant, insect, reptile, animal or whatever, and we list them on the board. I always encourage the more unusual or unexpected image, such as sunflowers rather than grass, or slugs rather than bees, and again I stress that we should be listing imagined as well as actual images and sounds. Once the students have brainstormed plenty of images and sounds for the board, and once we have started using comparisons (as in hearing "the spider/silent/as wisps of cream/melting in my coffee" in "The Silent Spider" by Kelly Prall, a sixth grader), we then write, the student writers either becoming the spider or following the spider around.

The Silent Spider

Hiding among my cucumber vines
I hear the spider
    silent
as wisps of cream
melting into coffee.
He waddles slowly, like a duck
over my rosy tomatoes,
over the bean plants,
across the rows.
He struggles over the plum-colored eggplants,
over the picket fence.
I follow, trying to be
as silent as he.
Over a fern leaf,
over a gopher's moist, cool nose,
    I follow,
over a daisy, onto his home,
like a hammock swiftly spun
      between
      two roses,
        delicate,
          soft,
           silent.

Kelly Prall, sixth grade

John Blazeck, a fourth grade writer, becomes a spider with metaphysical thoughts grounded in his very real garden in his poem, "I the Spider":

185

I the Spider

I the spider
  hear
    the wind blowing
      as a
        dangling
          string
    holds me from
      falling
      into
        a deep blue sea
        of roses.

And I the spider
  hear
    Time
      get trapped
      in my silver web
    and I wonder
      how does a heart
      stay red.

As the above poem shows, these spider poems are also good exercises to use for line break experimentation, to encourage the student writers to feel the rhythm in each line and to break the line, or move it about on the page accordingly. Marcus Blackwell, a seventh grader, also does this in his "I the Spider" poem"

      I the Spider
        quick
          and alert
            hear time
          like the flowing
          of the
        whispery
      waterfall,
    and, crawling
   over
the cucumbers,
    I hear
      its seeds
        like the pounding
      of the beautiful
African drums

```
            while
      the bronze antelope
                  is stalked
      by the shining gold
lioness--
        its rapidly beating
                 heart
                    slowly
                  coming to a halt.
```

A Third Variation on "Listening to Nature" (Beach, in This Instance) Poem, with the Additional Element of "Musical Accompaniment"

Since many students have been to a beach and have enjoyed the experience, it is a natural topic for a poem--the major danger being that they will fill the poem with cliched images and ideas. To avoid this, we stress the unique image and comparison once again in our brainstorming sessions, encouraging such images as Yang Hyo Park's "shell sounds" and "seaweed shaking" in his poem, "Walking down the Beach," or Bu Brendan Krueger's comparison, "Where time turns like the sparkling sea shells" in his poem, "Overhead."

And, again, the sense of hearing the real and the imagined is emphasized, as in the earlier "Listening Carefully in Nature"" and the "Quietest Moment" poems. An additional element which works well with these beach poems is to have the students refer to musical instruments, such as trombones, bass drums, or trumpets, for instance, and to have them draw comparisons between the beach images and the musical instruments. A pre-writing exercise for this would ask what musical instrument a conch shell sounds like, or a crab scuttling across the sand. The students enjoy this comparison-making exercise as much as they enjoy the "Spider in the Garden" poem, so there's plenty of enthusiasm and motivation to write.

Once we have a plentitude of images on the board ("clacking crayfish," "sinking starfish," the crabs' "black holes") and the students are making imaginative comparisons ("An octopus sprints away,/Leaving a trail of ink,/Like a broken pen," in Rachael Gaysek's "Walking down the Beach"), then we write, using a participial phrase--"Walking down the beach"-- to begin in order to put the students immediately into the scene.

Walking down the Beach

Walking down the beach
  I hear a harp
Being played harmoniously
  By the Pacific waves,
I see the dandelion yellow
  Of the sun
  As it shines
From the fin of a frantic dolphin
That leaps through the troughs

Of happiness,
   Of joy.

Walking down the beach
   I feel the chilling wind
      Wind around me
   With its many limbs,
   I see the crimson kite
      That flies
   High like a flute note
      Above
   The sunny swells while
The Ghost Grey crab scampers
      Across
   The golden sand,
      Ducks
      Suddenly
Into its black hole.

Lin-Z Holly, seventh grade

Walking down the Beach

   Walking down the beach
I hear children paddling in the sea,
   I catch crawfish and crabs
   and listen to shell sounds
   of round brown coconuts
hanging from the coconut trees

   Waves advance on the beach
   when I soak in the sea
      and hear Time
   like seaweed shaking--
   My spirit is cleansing
   and I love everything.

Yang Hyo Park, seventh grade

Walking down the Beach

I see the sea gulls squawking at the sun
   Like a choir that is off key

   I looked into the sea
   The waves area a huge fire

Taking over a building with flames

I see sea shells quivering
Like maracas shaking about

I see jellyfish floating above the waves
Like leaves falling off a giant oak

I see crabs clacking their claws
Like castanets under the ocean

Time sounds like butterflies
Flying under the hot setting sun
While the people pack up their umbrellas
Waiting for the next day of waves and fun

Suddenly I hear silence
As the moon rises to tell the day has ended
And the next day is soon to come.

Lauren Lorenzi, eighth grade

Or, in a poem that emphasizes both hearing and feeling, Erica Down, a fifth grader, presents a powerful, sensual ending.

On the Beach

On the beach,
        as quiet as a grain of sand,
        I listen carefully,
        hear the seashells clacking,
        the sand racing for the sea.

        I feel my muscles pull,
        I hear my conscience saying
            Go! Go! Get wet!
        while the seagulls eat
        popcorn, crumbs, crusts
            of bread,

        and I'm here listening
        to fish breathing
        and the whale's blowhole,

        feeling the water between my toes.

WRITING A POEM ABOUT NATURE FROM THE PERSPECTIVE OF A PERSONA IN A PRINT

This exercise asks the writers to assume the persona of a character in a print and to write from that perspective. Any print that has natural images in it will do, but one of my favorites, and one which several of the following student writings are about, is Alfred Sisley's *Banks of the Seine Near Bougival, 1873.*

Before writing, the students examine the print carefully and jot down images they find interesting, adding imagined images as they occur to them; I ask for a list of at least five images. Then we put several of the images on the board and talk about the colors, the play of light, the placement--and I once again remind them that they may use any of the words on the board if they get stuck in their writing. (I do not emphasize comparison-making for this exercise, for the focus remains on the image.) Then I ask them to begin by walking or standing along the (any color) river, and we write.

Nicole Metzger, a fifth grader, listens hard in her poem, "Standing by the Red River":

Standing by the Red River

Standing by the Red River
I can hear the reddish water
  rapidly moving
and I can feel the dead leaves
brushing against my legs
while others amble along the banks
waiting for the bright, hot sun
to go down.
Now all I can hear
is the leaves whistling
and the Red River skimming
over rocks,
and when I look up
at the pink and blue sky,
I see it's looking down on me.

Lea Librick, a fifth grader, emphasizes colors in her poem, "Walking along the Shore Banks":

Walking along the Shore Banks

Walking along the green river
an old man fishes
while a lady picks yellow marigolds
and the wind whistles among the leaves.

190

Looking along the shore
I see many people feeding brown
   bread to seagulls
that drift on white wings
while an old lady hangs her blue wash.
Now hawks soar under the purple sky
   where
it is getting late
and dusk is coming
like a pink comet.

Older students also write well by assuming the persona from a print and then writing, as is seen by the following poems which use Claude Monet's Terrace at Sainte-Adresse as a springboard. (The painting depicts four people sitting on a flower-filled terrace which faces out to an ocean busy with sailboats and steamships.)

Dreaming of Monet

Dreaming of pots of overflowing flowers,
bougainvillea spilling toward the sea,
gladiolus stretching glorious necks
toward the bluest skies, deep, bright
blue with no other name
and clouds all puff and drift.
Dreaming of flags flattening in Mediterranean wind
and sails billowing to and from places
I've never been, I sit here, on this terrace,
ivy-covered walls closing out other lives.
Only the curve of this cane-backed chair
curling around my body and the dress I wear,
white, like the air and my parasol
holding off the white heat,
with Max, gentle, still, silent,
finally free of frenetic tremors
stopped by the sun.
Dreaming of memories dulled by ocean waves
that beat, rippling against the sea wall.

Connie Weiss, high school teacher

A Second Variation on Writing a River Poem from a Print: "Remembering"

Once the students are comfortable creating imagistic poems about the Sisley (or any other) painting, I often try to involve them more personally in their poem writing by asking them to become a real or imagined persona in the painting and to "remember" some event that was meaningful to them, such as a special moment at a grandparent's house. This exercise helps blend the objective image of the painting with the more personal recollection, and it often results in a poignant "snapshot" poem, as may be seen in the following poems.

By the Purple River

Dear Mother, I remember
our walk by the purple river,
listening to the wind whiz
   through
the oak trees while father
fished in the glazing glitter.
Snap snap
his line tightened
and a shiny goldfish
was pulled up.
The tulips sensed the air
with a beautiful scent
and the houses stood
as still as a picture
till the purple river
   whispered
like a baby's cry
waking us.

Renee Gentile, fifth grade

Remember

  Standing by the sepia river,
I remember my Grandpa milking
   the cows on the farm
      in the dusk of the day.
   Meanwhile, in the house,
Grandma cooked Sunday supper,
with crispy brown turkey sizzling in
         the oven
and little ones played in the hay.

Now there are only the trees and the leaves
         of golden color,
and the waving lilies of the field,
         while
everyone gathers around the brown living room
      laughing about the old times.

Lisa Mendock, fifth grade

A Third Variation on Writing a Poem about Nature from the Perspective of a Persona in a Print: the Poem Expresses, through Its Selection of Images and Phrasing, One Major Emotion

For this exercise, which also blends image and emotion, I like to use Claude Monet's *Terrace at Sainte-Adresse.* The painting depicts four people sitting on a flower-filled terrace which faces out to an ocean busy with sailboats and steamers.

After we discuss the flowers (giving them names, exact shades of color, et cetera) and note the play of light on the ocean waves, including the ominous shadows, and after we make some interesting comparisons ("sorrows/that drift like lonely sailboats"), I ask the students to imaginatively become one of the four characters in the print and to convey an emotional state through their selection of images. Sometimes I will read previous student poems written to this exercise to help familiarize the students with the task, but usually this is not necessary and we just write. Following are some of the results.

Brooks Faure, a fourth-grader, captures her sense of sorrow in the young woman whom she sees as waiting for her husband to return from sea:

Waiting

I sit by the ocean
I say no words
longing for my husband
who has gone to sea
The ocean is as cold
as an ice cream cone
the waves are as white
as an old man's beard
I wait and wait
to get a letter
All it says is
sorrow

Edward Hui, a sixth grader, is not very content either, as he assumes the persona of the old man who sits on the patio, reflecting:

Staring at the Sea

Silently sitting in the stiff wicker chair,
I think about life, my life slowly wasting away.
I should be content like the serene irises,
or carefree as the waving magnolias,
but I'm not.
My life has ripples and ruffles rolling like the blue-teal

sea.

Nicole Adams, a seventh grader, captures her character's emotion--also the old man's--through her tight lines and diction:

Wait

A microscopic dot of perfect green
protected by fluffy magenta soldiers.
Time passes. Wind bellows.
Shadows grow.
Trapped inside,
many years surround me.
Filthy life leaks out,
painting the ragged edge
of the wet horizon.
Incoming ships.
Just wait.

A Fourth Variation of Writing about Nature by Having the Student Writers Assume the Persona of a Character: an Unassigned, Unexpected Process and Poem

Any print may serve as a starting point for this exercise, and I would like to include a final example to show the unique perspective and imaginative poem that may result. The following poem, for instance, is written by a student who has her mother assume the persona of Claude Monet as he/she paints *Poplars*. Again, the emphasis is on the natural images, although this student insists--as all writers do--on bringing her own personal concerns into the poem.

My Mother

As she adds a tint of green
to the poplars
in her painting,
she pictures herself
within the scene
standing on the pebbly beach
looking out across the weedy shore.
My father is also there,
thinking of a red Jaguar
polished and bright, that he
drives through Tennessee,
his tall form gazing
across the muddy river
until the leaves on the poplars
shake violently
like a loud alarm that awakens

my mother from her dreaming
to warn her that the cake
she is baking
is ready to be taken from the oven.
It is time to make dinner,
so she will not have the opportunity
to dream
until tomorrow
when she will paint the gray stormy sky.

Jenny Casagrande, eighth grade

CHAPTER NINETEEN: THE SENSORY NATURE POEM, WITH PRE-WRITING RESPONSE SHEETS FOR IMAGES AND COMPARISONS

THE SENSORY NATURE POEM, WITH PRE-WRITING RESPONSE SHEETS FOR IMAGES AND COMPARISONS

Note to teachers: Attached are three response sheets, each one asking for sensory information and comparisons. The answers the students write to the questions will provide them with information they may use while creating poems about their experience on any nature outing. (The students may create more than three sheets if they wish, but they should do at least three.)

The **Sensory Information Response Section** asks the students to use their five senses in describing their subject matter. Attached to this sheet are a Sense Word Chart and a Color Thesaurus that the students may refer to for guidance in selecting the best sensory word for their description.

The **Comparison Response Section** asks the students to make two kinds of comparisons: first, to compare their selected "thing" to something else in nature, and second, to compare their "thing" to something not in nature. For instance, "A pillbug looks like a tiny tank rolling over a hill," or "The brown leaf feels like my grandfather's hand." Such comparisons will provide the students with imaginative associations for their poems. Ten examples of student comparisons, five of each type, are provided in an appendix to the Comparison Response Sheet.

Finally, five student poems written about nature appear on the **Nature Poems** sheet. These poems demonstrate the use of sensory information and comparison making in young student writing.

The goal is poems to be written in class that will begin either with "Walking through the forest, I hear…," or "I, the spider, hear…," depending on the information the students gather. In either case, the students will be asked to use their sensory information and comparisons to develop their writing. "Walking through blue spring, I hear" and "I, the spider, hear" poems are included in the five student example poems on the Nature Poems sheet, so you and the students may see where this process might lead.

I am indebted to Gail Ghai, friend, fellow poet and teacher of poetry, for much of the information in this chapter, especially the Color Thesaurus and Sense Word Chart.

SENSORY INFORMATION RESPONSE SECTION

Select one thing you found during your walk in nature. It could be a rock, lump of clay, an insect, bird feather, or even a pillbug! Select words from the Sense Word Chart which best fits your description of its:

Shape:_____

_____

Touch:_____

_____

Smell:_____

_____

Sound:_____

_____

COMPARISON RESPONSE SECTION

Compare your selected "thing" to something in nature:

_____

_____

_____

_____

Compare your selected "thing" to something not in nature:

_____

_____

_____

SENSORY INFORMATION RESPONSE SECTION

Select a **second** thing you found during your walk in nature. Select words from the Sense Word Chart which best fits your description of its:

Shape:_____

_____

Touch:_____

_____

Smell:_____

_____

Sound:_____

_____

COMPARISON RESPONSE SECTION

Compare your selected "thing" to something in nature:

_____

_____

_____

Compare your selected "thing" to something not in nature:

_____

_____

_____

SENSORY INFORMATION RESPONSE SECTION

Select a **third** thing you found during your walk in nature. Select words from the Sense Word Chart which best fits your description of its:

Shape:_____

_____

Touch:_____

_____

Smell:_____

_____

Sound:_____

_____

COMPARISON RESPONSE SECTION

Compare your selected "thing" to something in nature:

_____

_____

_____

Compare your selected "thing" to something not in nature:

_____

_____

_____

SENSE WORD CHART

Sight Words:

round, flat, curved, wavy, ruffled, square, hollow, wide, narrow, crooked, lumpy, swollen, long, dotted, freckled, wrinkled, striped, shiny, sparkling, fiery, muddy, dark, old, worn, messy, cluttered, clean, tidy, tall, lean, muscular, healthy, fragile, pale, sickly, tiny, large, immense, perky, showy, elegant

Touch Words:

cool, cold, icy, lukewarm, warm, hot, steamy, sticky, damp, wet, slippery, spongy, mushy, oily, waxy, fleshy, rubbery, bumpy, crisp, silky, velvety, smooth, soft, woolly, furry, fuzzy, hairy, leathery, sandy, gritty, rough, sharp, thick, dry, thin, tender

Smell Words:

sweet, scented, fragrant, perfumed, fresh, earthy, piney, spicy, fishy, sharp, burnt, putrid, spoiled, sour, sickly, stagnant, musty, moldy, dry, damp, dank

Sound Words:

crash, thud, bump, boom, thunder, bang, roar, scream, screech, shout, yell, whistle, squawk, whine, bark, bleat, bray, rumble, grate, slam, clap, stomp, jangle, crackle, buzz, clink, hiss, snort, bellow, growl, whimper, stammer, snap, rustle, chime, laugh, gurgle, giggle, sing, hum, mutter, murmur, whisper, sigh, hush

Other Sense Words:

Add some of your own words:

COLOR THESAURUS

Beige　　　　buff, bamboo, biscuit, pearl, blond, ecru, linen, ivory, sandy, mushroom, ginger, porcelain, putty, taupe, champagne

Black inky, dark, pitch-black, ebony, lacquer, jet-black, lamp-black, obsidian, black-diamond, brunette, crow, onyx, zebra-wood, black walnut, raven, magpie, licorice, tea, midnight

Blue Biscay blue, storm-blue, volcano-blue, sapphire, Prussian blue, navy, Wedgwood blue, cobalt, bluebonnet, lapis lazuli, cornflower, blue jay, bluebird, indigo, hyacinth, bluebell, Mediterranean blue, powder blue, cyan, manganese, cerulean

Blue-green turquoise, teal, peacock, cerulean, verdigris, aqua, aquamarine, ultramarine, blue-de chine, robin's egg, Great blue heron, Aegean blue

Brown chocolate, cinnamon, walnut, nutmeg, mocha, coffee, cattail, cappuccino, pecan, burnt umber, henna, ochre, tan, chestnut, spice, caramel, fawn, caper, tobacco, tamarind

Gold flaxen, wheat, aureate, gilded, buckskin, citrine, Renaissance gold, citron, marigold, mica

Gray silver, chrome, glass, pewter, white-gold, sterling, tin, dove-gray, galena, patina, chrome, cloudy, smoke, mist, charcoal, manganese

Green emerald, jade, duckweed, malachite, mint, absinthe, chartreuse, Empire green, lime, Ming, kiwi, leaf, forest, Kelly green, broccoli, spinach, celery, cucumber, peacock, celadon, bloodstone, olivine, alexandrite, lacewing fly, brook trout, lichen, sap

Orange peach, apricot, coral, maple, adobe, magnolia, saffron, paprika, pumpkin, nectar, sepia, sienna, carotene, terracotta, rust, melon, mango, persimmon, orangutan, mimosa, iodine, smoky topaz, tangerine, Indian paintbrush, Bird-of-Paradise, marmalade, buckskin, copper

Pink rose, quartz, flesh, pastel pink, blush, rose pompadour, tulipwood, hunting pink, fuchsia, cyclamen, magenta, carnation, carnelian pink, plum, mauve, camellia, azalea, Roseate, spoonbill, flamingo, rosewood

Purple amethyst, violet, magenta, grape, lavender, mauve, lilac, fuchsia, cinnabar, vermilion, orchid, plum, iris, passion flower, fox grape

COLOR THESAURUS

Red rhubarb, ruby, garnet, scarlet, crimson, cardinal, cerise, oxblood, carnelian, henna, Mars, claret, burgundy, fruit punch, sanguine, rouge, vermilion, barn red, cranberry, pomegranate

White marble, marbleize, bleach, snow, milky, creamy, eggshell, onion, opal, cauliflower, pearl

Yellow canary, lemon, cider, grapefruit, primrose, turmeric, marigold, maize, daffodil, blonde, nasturtium, cadmium, sunflower, amber, butter, safflower, jonquil, Imperial yellow, lemonade, dandelion, banana, bronze, sulfur

Multicolor tonal, kaleidoscopic, prismatic, crewel, rainbow, confetti, potpourri, iridescent

COMPARISON RESPONSE SHEET APPENDIX WITH TEN EXAMPLES OF STUDENTS' COMPARISONS

Natural images compared to other natural images:

1. Snow sounds like
   a white horse in a field of daisies.

2. The falling red leaf looks like
   an ant dropping from the fragile
   petal of a violet.

3. The geese are like the flow
   of time across the blue sky.

4. The white rose smells like
   the sweet scent
   of my grandfather's tobacco.

5. The crow is as black
   as the charcoal black
   thunderstorm sky.

Natural images compared to non-natural images:

1. A yellow rose sounds like
   a school bus with
   fifty laughing kids.

2. The white rose looks like
   pictures drawn in chalk
   on the blackboard.

3. The red rose feels like
   our red-hot wood stove
   on a freezing winter night.

4. The snow looks like
   a white sheet under a Christmas tree,
   no presents at all.

5. The ruby shines like
   a beautiful cardinal
   pecking on a black Mercedes.

Walking through Blue Spring,

   I hear
turkeys sounding like trumpets
and snails crawling slow
   as time
over stony mountains.
   The air
smells fresh as apples
and the tree bark
   is rough as a rock.
Watch out, the roses
are ready to sprout!
   I'll
walk through this spring
   anytime!

Joel Werner, Fourth Grade

I the Spider

hear
   the wind blowing
         as a dangling string
   holds me
     from falling
into a deep blue sea of roses.

And I
   the spider
     hear time
        get trapped
        in my silver web
      and I wonder
        how does a heart
        stay red.

John Blazeck, Fourth Grade

The Willow

In the woods,
as silent as a fly,
I heard a willow
as it grew and grew,
its lovely arms
looking more and more
like tentacles
turning orange
in the setting sun.
Listening carefully,
I heard field mice
walking, climbing
wheat stalks thin
as thread. Soon,
they said, the willow
will come alive
and dance
soft as a cloud
in the sky.

Melissa Tavares, Fourth Grade

Dad

The quietest moment of my life
is just before I drop to sleep
and I hear the snaps of sparks
in the downstairs fireplace.
I hear the bullfrog croaking in the lake,
and the crackling caterpillars
munching heartily on leaves
until they are all gone.
I hear the chirps of crickets
like fiddlers in the night…
all is quiet as a leaf
drifting to the ground.

Jeff Krouse, Fifth Grade

On the Beach

On the beach,
        as quiet as a grain of sand,
        I listen carefully,
        hear the seashells clacking,
        the sand racing for the sea.

        I feel my muscles pull,
        I hear my conscience saying

        Go! Go! Get wet!
        while the seagulls eat
        popcorn, crumbs, crusts
            of bread,

        and I stay here listening
        to fish breathing
        and the whale's blowhole,

        feeling the water between my toes.

Erica Down, Fifth Grade

REVISION CHECKLIST

Verlaine: "You never finish a poem, you abandon it."

1. Be wary of, say, first and last three or four lines; they tend to be introductions and conclusions.

2. Sharpen images; make as authentic and vivid as possible.

3. Sharpen discourse; make sure you're making the general statement with interesting language.

4. Delete cliches, usual language.

5. Don't invert syntax unnecessarily.

6. Change any word that seems to unintentionally "clang," musically or logically; use thesaurus.

7. Be aware of Anglo Saxon and Latinate language use and revise accordingly. For example, a Latinate term in a poem that's primarily Anglo Saxon, will be emphasized, and vice versa.

8. Listen to the rhythm of the poem's best lines; make sure you have a distinguishable rhythm throughout poem, with no (unintentional) prosaic sections.

9. Revise line lengths for enjambment and end-stop, always listening to the rhythm of the lines.

10. Try switching lines around for more unusual associations; stronger associations often occur when you delete material and bridge the gap.

11. Change tense, person, to see what different effects you get, both musically and logically

12. Keep ONE focus (cut extraneous material) as in a typical Gary Snyder poem or MANY foci, as in a Pablo Neruda poem, but be sure you know why you are doing what you are doing.

13. Be sure poem ends musically as well as logically.

14. Let the poem speak; don't impose your will, what you want, on the poem. The poem always knows better than you do!